BELIEFS, BEHAVIOUR AND EDUCATION

Beliefs, Behaviour and Education

ROGER STRAUGHAN

CASSELL

Cassell Educational Limited
Artillery House
Artillery Row
London SW1P 1RT

First published 1989

British Library Cataloguing in Publication Data
Straughan, Roger, *1941–*
  Beliefs, behaviour and education.
  1. Moral education
  I. Title
  370.11′4   .

  ISBN 0–304–31862–0 (hardback)
        0–304–31860–4 (paperback)

Phototypeset by Input Typesetting Ltd, London
Printed and bound in Great Britain by
Biddles Ltd, Guildford and King's Lynn

To Compton Mackenzie, a spirited advocate of moral courage.

Contents

Preface

Schopenhauer has been described as 'the philosopher with an obsession for the will'. I sympathize with him, as my own more limited obsession has been for some years with the problem of weakness of will and its educational implications. In a number of books and articles I have tried to show how the relationship between our judgments and our actions, or our beliefs and our behaviour, forms a key element in many current educational concerns. As these writings are widely scattered, sometimes in rather inaccessible publications, and as many of the issues which they raise are coming to ever-increasing prominence in educational debate, it seemed a good idea to gather together some of this work in one volume, supplemented by new material where appropriate. This has also given me the opportunity for a full revision, with the result that none of the following chapters has ever appeared previously in its present form.

Two general points need to be made at the outset. Firstly, this book is not designed to present a developing, cumulative argument, leading to final conclusions. Each chapter stands on its own feet and concentrates on a specific educational question, while at the same time serving also to illustrate one facet of the broader problem upon which the whole book pivots. A single chapter can thus be read or discussed in isolation if required, though the breadth of the context in which it can be located will not then be fully appreciated. Secondly, many of the chapters are relatively (and mercifully) short, as their aim is more often to raise, reformulate and explore problems than to argue towards conclusive answers. To encourage readers to engage in this Socratic process, therefore, each chapter ends with a few further questions for reflection or discussion.

Acknowledgements

As explained in the Preface, none of the chapters of this book has previously appeared in its present form. However, permission has been granted to use and adapt previously published material for the following chapters:

Chapters 1 and 2: permission granted by the Philosophy of Education Society of Great Britain for material reprinted from the *Journal of Philosophy of Education*, vols **16**(1) and **12**.

Chapters 4 and 7: permission granted by the Open University Press for material reprinted from Spiecker, B. and Straughan, R. (eds) (1988) *Philosophical Issues in Moral Education and Development* and from *Can We Teach Children to be Good? Basic Issues in Moral, Personal and Social Education* (1988).

Chapters 5 and 8: permission granted by the *Journal of Moral Education* for material reprinted from vols **4**(3) and **12**(3).

Chapter 9: permission granted by Routledge for material reprinted from Entwistle, N. (ed.) (1989) *Handbook of Educational Ideas and Practices*.

Chapter 10: permission granted by John Wiley & Sons Ltd for material reprinted from Weinreich-Haste, H. and Locke, D. (eds) (1983) *Morality in the Making*.

Chapter 11: permission granted by Falmer Press Ltd for material reprinted from Modgil, S. and Modgil, C. (eds) (1986) *Lawrence Kohlberg: Consensus and Controversy*.

Introduction

Education, like most complex human activities, is full of problems. Before we can start to solve or even tackle any of these, it is essential to try to classify and categorize them in order to see which problems raise similar issues or stem from similar conflicts. This exercise is crucial in clarifying our educational thinking and in avoiding the waste of time and effort which results if we treat all problems as if they were completely new and unique, or to use more fashionable terminology 'one-off' and 'free-standing'.

This book is concerned with one particular set of educational problems, which at first glance may not appear to be obviously related because they can and do occur in a variety of different contexts. The following are some random examples of this set.

1. Tim learns from his health education course at school about the dangers of smoking. This course explains the reasons supporting Government health warnings contained in cigarette advertisements, such as 'Smoking can cause heart disease' and 'More than 30,000 people die each year in the UK from lung cancer'. Tim's class also discusses during the course the high financial cost of being a cigarette smoker, some social and aesthetic objections to smoking and the possible harmful effects on non-smokers of being exposed to smoke from other people's cigarettes. Tim appreciates the evidence that is presented, and in discussion expresses his concern at the alarming statistics. Yet on the way home from school he is offered a

cigarette by a friend 'to see what it's like', accepts it and soon becomes a regular, surreptitious smoker.

2. Tina is an able child with no particular learning difficulties or emotional problems. She is capable of producing work in most subject areas that is well above the average standard for her age group. Her school reports, however, tend with monotonous regularity to present variations on the familiar themes of 'Could do much better' and 'Doesn't try hard enough'. In discussion with her teachers and her parents Tina admits that the comments are justified. She knows that she often does not achieve the results she could do, and that she is unlikely to be able to pursue the career she is hoping for if she does not work harder. She promises to make more effort next term – but her good intentions are somehow not enough and the next report shows no sign of any improvement. ·

3. Tony is a student teacher on teaching practice. He has learnt from his tutors and from school staff the importance of setting the right tone at the beginning of each lesson and of insisting on the undivided attention of every pupil before starting on a new piece of work. He fully understands the reasons why this will make his teaching more effective. Nevertheless, on entering the classroom of the dreaded 3H on Monday morning he notes with a sinking heart a group of trouble-makers whispering and sniggering ominously at the back of the room, and feels that he cannot be bothered to intervene and exert his authority. He starts to talk to the pupils at the front of the class and is soon fighting a losing battle; his teaching has increasingly little impact and disorder rapidly spreads.

These examples, which could be multiplied indefinitely, share a basic common factor: each involves a certain kind of failure or weakness, which in turn stems from a certain kind of conflict. It is these failures, weaknesses and conflicts which lie at the heart of this book and also in a rather strange sense at the heart of education.

Education essentially aims to alter both mental and physical behaviour. Successful education must, by definition, affect how people think and judge and assess and deliberate, how they draw conclusions and make decisions, and how they act. This is achieved largely through the medium of reasons. The learner is subjected to various experiences which are designed to increase his knowledge, understanding, appreciation and sensitivity. He may, for example, be taught, instructed, corrected, questioned, given explanations and demonstrations, set problems, or led to make discoveries; and these and other educational methods are 'rational' in the sense that part of their purpose is to develop within the learner the awareness that there are good reasons both for believing certain things rather than others and for doing certain things rather than others. So education effects its changes indirectly by gradually increasing the learner's comprehension of various kinds of reason in the hope that these will influence the ways in which he thinks and acts; in this respect it is unlike other methods of changing behaviour, such as conditioning, which operate directly upon the learner's responses without needing to depend upon the mediating function of reasons.

But because education works in this indirect way it suffers from one serious weakness; its successful outcome is less certain than that of more direct methods, and so can never be guaranteed. The problem which lies at the heart of education, and also at the heart of this book, stems from this uncertainty, for it is concerned with the nature of the relationship between theory and practice, between judgment and action, between beliefs and behaviour. This problem can be stated briefly as follows. Education aims to produce a certain 'rational' state of mind in the learner by bringing him to acknowledge the validity of reasons, but this state of mind may have a greater or a lesser effect upon how the person actually behaves. His reasoning may or may not remain at a theoretical level; his judgments may or may not be translated into action; his beliefs may or may not guide his behaviour.

This educational problem about how 'rational' beliefs and judgments can be more closely linked to the learner's behaviour arises in many different contexts – in any context, in fact, in which it is possible for the pupil on the one hand to believe that there are good reasons why he ought to do something (or not do something), yet on the other hand not to act upon that belief. The examples of Tim, Tina and Tony given above are all of this kind.

We often attribute such failures to act in accordance with our beliefs to 'weakness of will': we do not do what we believe we ought to do, or we do what we believe we ought not to do, because we are in some sense not strong enough to do otherwise.

In some cases this lack of strength is thought to be a specifically 'moral' failing, and we then sometimes speak of 'moral weakness' – e.g. a boy may believe it is wrong for him to remain a member of a gang which bullies younger children, yet be afraid to withdraw. Frequently, however, the failure does not relate to an obviously 'moral' issue – e.g. a girl may fail to check her work for careless mistakes, as she knows she should.

As I have previously attempted elsewhere to offer a detailed analysis of so-called 'weakness of will' and its educational significance,[1] I shall not repeat those arguments at length in this book. Instead, a more indirect approach will be adopted. Each chapter will focus upon a different educational issue, all of which share, however, a common feature, in that they illustrate a variety of problems all arising from the relationship between beliefs and behaviour (or judgment and action) and explore the educational significance of those problems, many of which are highly topical in the light of recent ministerial expressions of concern about pupils' behaviour in and out of school and about their moral and academic standards.

Thus, the first and most general section begins by examining the nature and function of rules and analysing what appears to be happening when children learn to follow rules, for here is clearly an area where children's beliefs and judgments (that X is a sensible rule) may at times seem to conflict with their actual behaviour. This is followed in Chapter 2 by a closer scrutiny of motivational factors and their effect on children's behaviour; the argument here suggests that children's wants, because of their tight logical connection with reasons for action, should be given more educational emphasis at both the theoretical and the practical levels. Finally, in this opening section the controversial question of educational standards is tackled in a way which further exemplifies how disparities can easily arise between expectation and practice.

The second section concentrates more specifically upon what is probably the most obvious area in which educational problems about beliefs and behaviour come to mind – moral education. Chapter 4 sets the scene by showing how the relationship between judgment and action must lie at the heart of morality and of moral education, and by outlining the problems posed for moral education by the phenomenon of so-called 'moral weakness'. Teachers and researchers concerned with moral education and moral development often make use of hypothetical moral situations to simulate 'real-life' moral dilemmas, and in Chapter 5 it is claimed that this approach will have serious limitations if a simple and direct connection is assumed to exist between hypothetical and 'real life' moral judgments. A range of teaching methods which might be used to combat 'moral weakness' is discussed in Chapter 6, while in Chapter 7 the pedagogical problems are approached from another angle which highlights the distinctions between teaching that . . . , teaching how . . . and teaching to. . . . The section ends with a consideration of how moral values can be assessed and a questioning of the assumption that they can unfailingly be identified in overt behaviour.

The third and final section takes the influential work of Lawrence Kohlberg as its focus in order to re-examine some of the main issues to have emerged so far and to raise some new ones. Chapter 9 offers a brief, general account of some recent developmental theories which have implications for the relationship between beliefs and behaviour in both the moral and the religious areas. This is followed by the two concluding chapters in which Kohlberg's account of moral judgment and action is investigated and criticized in some detail in the light of the issues which will have emerged in earlier chapters.

The contents of this book, then, while being extremely varied, are also closely interconnected by their common underlying theme. Indeed, it is the range of practical educational issues permeated by the same theoretical problem which has prompted me to produce this collection. Many may disagree with my interpretation of the theoretical problem about beliefs and behaviour, and consequently with the educational conclusions which I draw from it. Yet I hope that the following chapters will show at least that all educators need to have worked out a considered view of the relationship between judgment and action, for that relationship inevitably lies at the heart of their educational practice.

REFERENCE

(1) Straughan, R. (1982) *I Ought to, But . . . A Philosophical Approach to the Problem of Weakness of Will in Education* (Windsor: NFER-Nelson).

Section One

Chapter 1

What's the Point of Rules?

The educational value and status of rules is a subject which tends to provoke strong feelings and heated reactions from parents, teachers, politicians – and children. This is because rules suggest control, constraint, discipline and authority – concepts which are often the source of social and political controversy. Rules also offer an appropriate starting-point for the opening chapter of this book, for they are clearly related both to people's beliefs about what is right and wrong, acceptable and unacceptable, and to their subsequent behaviour. The mere existence of a set of rules, however, is no guarantee, of course, that those rules will be acted upon, even by those who may claim to accept and support them.

There are many questions that can be asked about rules, and the title of this chapter might suggest that one of several equally tedious and predictable lines of argument is to be inflicted on the reader – perhaps a libertarian attack on the practice of getting children to conform to rules, or a traditionalist defence of that practice, or an attempt to reconcile these two positions by dissolving the grounds of the apparent dispute.

The reader can, however, be reassured that none of these familiar fates awaits him. I am not concerned here so much with the justifiability or desirability of children's rule-following behaviour as with the problem of what it actually means for children to learn, follow and obey rules, and what precisely is going on in these activities. It is in fact the *logical* point of rules that is being questioned in the title, for by probing the nature of rules I hope to show that it is possible to entertain serious doubts about whether they have much logical point at all, whether the notion of rule-following does any distinctive or useful conceptual work, and whether children can ever be said, strictly speaking, to learn to follow rules as such.

In my first section, then, I shall illustrate how these doubts can arise when we look more closely at examples of what we usually assume to be rule-following behaviour, while the second section will suggest a possible solution to the puzzle which retains an important logical and educational function for the learning of rules by children.

OBEYING A RULE BECAUSE IT'S A RULE

Children have to learn a great number of rules. Rules are an essential element in our social lives and experience, for they shape and indeed constitute all of the social institutions and activities in which we participate as self-aware, social creatures. Children could hardly grow up into anything resembling what we understand by human beings without learning all kinds of rules – social, moral, legal, institutional, and so on.

Yet to make this obvious point presupposes that we have a clear idea of what is meant by saying that children can learn to follow rules – but what exactly does this entail? One cannot properly be said to have learned a rule, or to be following or obeying a rule, unless one knows that there is such a rule. There may, for example, be a rule against picking flowers from the beds in the park, but the mere fact that a toddler refrains from picking flowers does not necessarily mean that he has learned that rule or is obeying it. The idea of picking the flowers may never have entered his head, or he may have been steered well away from the flower beds by his mother to avoid temptation. Merely to act in the way that a rule prescribes, then, is clearly not sufficient to constitute a case of conscious rule-following; dogs are even less likely than toddlers to spend their time in the park picking flowers, but we do not normally think that their abstinence in this respect qualifies as an example of obeying a rule. As Warnock puts it, '. . . I do not *obey* that rule if I do not know of it, just as, if I do what the policeman told me to, I do not obey him if I could not hear, or could not understand, what he said to me'.[1]

So in order to follow a rule a child must be aware that there *is* such a rule; but this in turn seems to require that he also has some idea of what a rule actually is. Let us suppose that at an infant school there is a rule that coats are always to be hung up on pegs in the cloakroom. The teacher of the reception class might use a variety of methods to try to ensure that all the children in her class conform to this rule. She might, for instance, say on the children's first day at school, 'Now I want you all to hang your coat on one of those pegs and not leave it lying on the lockers, please'. Or she might say, 'Don't leave your coat on the locker; hang it up on a peg!' Or she might say on the second day to Johnny, with all the other children listening, 'Don't you remember, Johnny, what I said about hanging your coat up?' Or she might, after a couple of weeks of such reminders, meaningfully pick up Johnny's discarded coat, fix him with a baleful glare, and without a word forcibly propel him towards a vacant peg.

Now in none of these cases is the teacher necessarily conveying to the children that there is a *rule* about hanging up coats, nor giving them any idea of what rules are, however successful she may be in achieving an immaculately tidy cloakroom. What she is doing in the above examples is either to express her own wishes to the children, or to give them orders, or to remind them of those orders, or to use psychological and physical coercion; and the children in hanging up their coats are simply doing what the teacher either wants or instructs or reminds or forces them to do. None of this amounts to the teaching or learning of *rules*, despite the fact that the teacher is producing behaviour which *conforms* to the rule.

What the teacher is failing to do by these means is, of course, to give the children any indication of certain logically necessary features of rules – in particular, *their non-particular and non-personal nature*. Rules are non-particular in that they refer to a general class of behaviour rather than to a specific action on a specific occasion. Thus, the cloakroom rule would be 'Coats are to be hung up on pegs', applying it to *all* children in the class on *all* occasions; telling the children to hang up their coats today, or forcing Johnny to hang up his coat on Friday does nothing to convey the *generality* of rules. Rules also are non-personal in that it is strictly irrelevant who enunciates and enforces the rule, and how he or she feels about it. As Durkheim put it, '. . . the rule ceases to be itself if it is not impersonal, and if it is not represented as such to people's minds'.[2] So by saying, 'I want you all to hang up your coat' and by issuing personal instructions to that effect, the teacher is getting the children to do what *she* wants or tells them to do, and not what the rule impersonally requires.

How, then, can these necessary features of rules be taught to young children in such a way that they come to appreciate the difference between rules on the one hand and requests, orders, instructions and threats on the other? If children's learning has to start from the concrete, the particular and the personal, how does the notion of non-particular, non-personal rules start to develop? How is the jump made from believing that X ought to be done because the teacher *wants* it to be done to believing that X ought to be done because there is a rule that requires it?

There is a logical as well as a psychological dimension to these questions which has attracted the attention of philosophers of education. The standard answer which they have tended to offer has been in terms of 'giving reasons'. Teachers and parents, it is often argued, can only wean children away from highly personal-ized forms of control towards a more impersonal conception of authority and rules by giving *reasons* for their instructions. Thus, our infant teacher would place less and less emphasis upon the fact that it is *she* who wants the coats to be hung up neatly and *she* who is giving the instruction, and more and more emphasis upon the *reasons* why it is in general a good thing to hang coats up (e.g. because they are not so easily lost that way, they keep their shape better, they dry out more quickly when wet, etc.) By this method, the argument goes, children gradually acquire the notion of generalized, non-personal reasons which justify or require particular forms of behaviour, regardless of who says so, and thereby learn to follow rules *as rules*.

Unfortunately, however, on closer inspection this apparently simple answer fails to provide an adequate solution to the problem of how children learn to follow rules. We have now distinguished two means by which children's behaviour may be influenced – either via the personal control and charisma of the teacher (or parent), or via an understanding of non-personal reasons for action seen by the child as justificatory. But in neither case does anything that can properly be called rule-following seem to be going on. In the first case we have already seen that acting merely to please someone, or to avoid her disapproval, has nothing to do with understanding and following rules as such; while in the second case, if children have *already* reached the stage of recognizing that there are non-personal, justificatory reasons for doing X rather than Y, then they have passed beyond mere rule following, and it is misleading to describe their autonomous, rational behaviour in terms of merely obeying rules. The child who hangs his wet coat up because he appreciates that it will dry out more quickly that way is doing this because he sees a good reason for it, not because there happens to be a rule about it. So getting children to appreciate reasons cannot be claimed to bridge the gap between personal control and non-personal rules, for once the child realizes that there can be justificatory reasons for action, it will be *reasons* that justify or require his doing X, not the fact that there is a rule about X. To quote Warnock again, '. . . there will be no need to make a rule requiring that to be done which people will anyway see that there is good reason to do'.[3]

Is the notion of learning to follow rules, therefore, a redundant one? Suspicions that it might be increase when we examine what John Wilson has to say on this subject in his discussion of the concept of discipline, which he claims involves obeying rules *because they are authoritative*. 'This is importantly different', he says, 'from obeying them because they happen to issue from an admired source; but it is also importantly different from obeying them because they are good rules, or sensible rules, or rules required for the purposes of the institution . . .'[4] Wilson believes there to be 'clearly a particular concept at stake here: roughly, the notion of *obedience to established and legitimate authorities as such*. . . . To accept rules as authoritative, in the sense required for discipline, consists partly in accepting them as *reasons for action*, and this is verified by whether, in the practical situations involved, the motivating thought is something like "it's a rule" rather than anything else . . .'[5]

The distinctions which Wilson draws here are similar to those which we have been examining, and his 'particular concept' of discipline is closely connected with the elusive notion of rule-following with which this chapter is concerned. But Wilson does not succeed in mapping out a logically distinctive or coherent middle-ground between the two alternatives of obeying a personal, 'admired source' on the one hand, and recognizing the justificatory, rational force of 'good or sensible rules' on the other.

The problem lies in the idea of obeying rules *because they are authoritative*, and of obeying established and legitimate authorities *as such*. How does a child come to recognize a rule as authoritative or an authority as legitimate? Not, according to Wilson, by merely obeying an 'admired source', nor by acknowledging that there are reasons which make the authority's rules 'good or sensible', for the 'particular concept' of rule-following discipline is distinct from both of these. But what then is left? The notion of obeying rules or authorities *as such* turns out to be literally vacuous. A child can *either* conform to the edicts of some personal source of power and influence, *or* he can appreciate the reasons which justify an edict and accordingly make it authoritative rather than merely authoritarian. In neither case, however, is he obeying rules or authorities *as such*, for in the former he is simply doing as he is told, perhaps with no idea of what constitutes a rule or a legitimate authority, while in the latter he is doing what he sees there to be good and sensible reasons for doing, which is precisely what Wilson wants to exclude from his 'particular concept' of discipline.

It appears then that children logically cannot (and so, of course, in practice do not) learn to obey rules as such – i.e. simply because they are seen to *be* rules. Any alleged example of this phenomenon is more accurately to be classified under one or other of the two explanatory categories of reasons for action which Wilson refers to and which this chapter has so far illustrated. Even accounts of how and why children follow the rules of a game (which might be thought to provide a counter-example) turn out to be classifiable in either of these two ways, rather than as obeying a rule 'because it's a rule'. The responses of Piaget's marbles-playing children, for instance, do not as is commonly assumed support a 'rule-following as such' interpretation. Piaget's subjects follow the rules either because some 'admired source' such as older children, parents, God, or the Town Council pro- claims them,[6] or because there are seen to be good reasons for following them if one wants to play the game properly – ' "So as not to be always quarrelling," says Ross, "you must have rules and then play properly." '[7] Thus, the child at first, in Piaget's words, 'receives commands from older children (in play) and from adults (in life), and . . . respects older children and parents',[8] while at a later stage 'the interventions of reason' result from a process of 'progressive co-operation'.[9] Even here, then, children cannot be said to be obeying rules *as such*, and our two explanatory categories are quite adequate to cover such examples.

So what *is* the logical point of rules? Having initially maintained that children must necessarily learn to follow all kinds of rules in order to develop as social, human beings, I have now reached the paradoxical position of questioning whether rules have much logical point at all, or at least whether there is any conceptual room for Wilson's 'particular concept' of rule-following discipline. It would, though, be premature to draw the conclusion that rule-following is a wholly redundant notion which can consequently be ignored by teachers and parents. In the following section I shall therefore try to be more constructive in suggesting that rules do indeed serve an important educational function.

THE EDUCATIONAL FUNCTION OF RULES

What I have attempted to reveal as vacuous and incoherent in the previous section is not the idea of rule-following itself but that of learning to obey a rule *as such*, 'because it's a rule'. A child must have some rudimentary understanding of what rules are before he can properly be said to be obeying one, but it does not follow from this that his reason for obeying the rule must be 'because it's a rule', nor that he must *learn* to obey it for that reason. It is only when rule-following is interpreted as obeying rules because they are rules that it becomes a conceptual non-starter.

For what other reasons, then, might children learn that rules are to be obeyed? Two different types of reason for action have, by implication, been distinguished in the previous section – those which motivate and those which justify. I shall refer to this distinction at some length in later chapters, the main point being, briefly, that in saying that A's reason for doing X was Y, we may be using Y to refer *either* to those factors in the situation which *motivate* A to do X, *or* to those factors which A considers *justify* or *require* him doing X. Quite often these two types of reason for action may coincide in cases where one positively *wants* to do that which one believes one *ought* to do (possibly *because* one believes one ought to), but on some occasions they may not, and we then find ourselves faced with distasteful duties and obligations which we

believe we ought to discharge without feeling any desire or inclination to do so. The phenomenon of so-called 'weakness of will'
arises in such contexts, where there is a conflict between motivational and justificatory reasons for action.

This distinction accords well with the account of children's
behaviour given in the previous section. If a child obeys the
teacher by hanging up his coat because of the personal control
and influence which she exercises, he is acting for motivational
reasons – i.e. he wants to please the teacher, or avoid her disapproval. But if he appreciates that there are good and sensible
reasons of a non-personal kind for hanging one's coat up – e.g.
because it keeps its shape better that way, dries out more quickly,
etc. – these will be justificatory reasons, which may not on all
occasions actually motivate the child to hang his coat up if there
is some stronger motivation operative – e.g. the need to dash into
the classroom to avoid being late and getting into trouble.

How then might the learning of rules fit into this general picture? If we judge it to be educationally desirable that children
should gradually come to feel the force of justificatory reasons,
as distinct from reasons which refer solely to their personal likes
and dislikes and their wants and fears, then learning to follow rules
may perhaps fulfil a crucial educational developmental function in
this respect. To tell children, for example, that there is a school
rule against running down the stairs and to enforce this prescription *as a rule* seems to link both the motivational and the justificatory aspects of reasons for action. The fact that there *is* such a
rule and that it is enforced provides a sanction against breaking
it and consequently a motive for not breaking it, because the
children will normally want to avoid the sanction. At the same
time, to announce and enforce this *as a rule* indicates that it
does not represent the arbitrary will of an individual teacher, but
reasons of a more general, non-personal kind (even if they are
not fully spelled out) – e.g. more accidents occur when children
run down stairs than when they walk. Experiencing rules in this
way may well be the only means by which children can develop
from a stage where motivational reasons alone are operative to
one where reasons are seen to justify as well as motivate.

I am suggesting, then, that rules may act as a temporary bridging device, serving to link in children's minds two distinct forms
of reasoning; but there remains the problem of how young chil-

dren can be taught to understand and follow rules, as distinct from merely doing as they are told, at a time when they have little or no grasp of justificatory reasons. How can teachers and parents start to give children some idea of the non-personal and non-particular features of rules which may be crucial in weaning them away from a dependence upon purely motivational reasons for action towards an appreciation of justificatory factors?

An important clue can perhaps be found in Piaget's emphasis upon the *respect* felt by children for those adults whose commands they accept, and also in Wilson's mention of rules issuing from an *admired* source. Despite their logically non-personal nature, rules must nevertheless in practice emanate from some source, and for young children that source is very likely to be an adult with whom they have a close personal relationship. They will first encounter rules, therefore, in an interpersonal context, and whether a particular rule is obeyed or not will depend initially upon motivational factors associated with the rule-giving adult – e.g. whether or not the child likes, fears, wants to please him, etc. At this early stage the child will simply be doing (or not doing) as he is told, but unless he remains permanently at the level of reacting mechanically and unthinkingly to commands, he will soon begin to trust (or mistrust) the rule-giver, as a result partly of what happens when he does as he is told, and partly of his view of the total personal relationship which he is developing with the rule-giver. He will accordingly gradually gain (or lose) confidence in the rule-giver *as a source of prescriptions*, and the basis of this trust (or mistrust) will start to become justificatory rather than purely motivational. One comes to *trust* another person not because one likes or fears him, but because one accepts that there are consistently good reasons backing what the other says and does. Trust and confidence develop only when they are thought to be *justified* by a reliable track record. As young children cannot at first appreciate, however, when a rule-giver has good reasons which justify what he prescribes, their progress towards a justificatory form of reasoning will have to start from the motivational impetus of a personal relationship with the pre-scribing adult, and proceed via a more generalized conception of trust and confidence in that person as a respected rule-giver.

This proposed continuum supports my suggestion that rule-following occupies an intermediate, linking position (both logically and developmentally) between the two distinct types of reason for action, but that at no stage do children follow rules purely because they are rules. Learning to follow rules, as distinct from doing as one is told on the one hand, and appreciating justificatory reasons on the other, would seem to go hand in hand with the development of trust and confidence in a prescribing adult, which will initially have some personal, motivational basis, but which also contains the seeds for the later emergence of non-personal, justificatory reasons for action. This, then, is the logical and educational point of rules.

One final methodological implication for the teacher and parent follows from all this. The non-personal, non-particular features of rules and of justificatory reasons for action will be more easily conveyed to children if the rule-giving authority is seen to be fair and consistent. Fairness and consistency will be best demonstrated if on the one hand the rule-giver clearly applies the rule impartially to all who come within its jurisdiction, regardless of whether he is known to like them or not, and if on the other hand the individual child is taught that the rule applies to him all the time and under all (reasonable) circumstances, regardless of how he and the rule-giver happen to be feeling on particular occasions. Thus, a school rule against running down the stairs must be shown to apply to *all* the children and be upheld by *all* the teachers, and the individual child must learn that the rule applies to him on *all* occasions and not just when the head teacher is watching. This is not, of course, to deny that there can be extenuating circumstances or justifiable exceptions to rules, nor that it can be educationally valuable to discuss such matters with children; but the fact remains that a child will be unable to escape from the arbitrary particularity of 'doing what Miss X says', until he comes to appreciate that there can be such things as rules, which are fairly and consistently administered in a non-personal way by trusted authorities.[10]

NOTES AND REFERENCES

(1)   Warnock, G. J. (1971) *The Object of Morality* (London: Methuen), p. 48.

(2)   Durkheim, E. (1925) *Moral Education* (New York: Free Press of Glencoe), p. 156.

(3) *Op. cit.*, p. 46.
(4) Wilson, J. (1977) *Philosophy and Practical Education* (London: Routledge & Kegan Paul), p. 38.
(5) Ibid., p. 40.
(6) Piaget, J. (1932) *The Moral Judgment of the Child* (London: Routledge & Kegan Paul), p. 52.
(7) Ibid., p. 63.
(8) Ibid., p. 101.
(9) Ibid., p. 103.
(10) I am grateful to members of the W. Midlands and Merseyside branches of the Philosophy of Education Society of Great Britain for their helpful comments on an earlier version of this chapter.

FURTHER QUESTIONS FOR CONSIDERATION

(1) Do you agree that teachers need to teach young children what rules are? Do parents need to do the same?

(2) Can you give sense to the notion of learning to obey a rule 'because it's a rule'? Do you agree with Wilson that there is 'a particular concept at stake here'?

(3) What is the relationship between discipline and rule-following?

(4) What dangers are inherent in children learning to obey rules which issue from an 'admired source'?

(5) Can rules exist without sanctions? What are the educational implications of this?

(6) If a child breaks a rule, does it necessarily mean that he does not 'accept' it? What sorts of reasons do children have for breaking rules?

(7) How important is it for teachers and parents to distinguish between moral and non-moral rules?

Chapter 2

Children's Wants

If the subject of rule-following considered in the previous chapter has an authoritarian ring about it, the title of this chapter appears to redress the balance by focusing upon the much more 'liberal'-sounding, 'child-centred' notion of children's wants. Does it matter what children want from the educational point of view? Should children's wants be viewed as a help or a hindrance in the educational process? Is it not perhaps dangerous to pay undue attention to children's wants, particularly in the area of *moral* education? These are some of the questions to be investigated in this chapter.

Educationalists in general and philosophers of education in particular have devoted a lot of attention over recent years to the notion of children's needs but very little to the notion of children's wants. The standard procedure of philosophers has usually been to dispose summarily of wants by contrasting them briefly with needs; a child may not want what he needs nor need what he wants, the argument usually goes, and the normative nature of statements about children's needs makes them educationally and morally more significant than descriptive statements about children's wants and, consequently, a more promising quarry for the philosopher of education.[1]

Claims for the educational importance of children's wants are normally assumed to have to rely either upon wholly 'child-centred' arguments (to the effect that everything which emanates from the child, including his wants, is educationally valuable *because* it emanates from the child), or upon wholly 'instrumental/motivational' arguments (to the effect that a child's wants can be effectively used in arousing and sustaining his interest in learning).

By contrast, in what is to follow I shall, on the one hand, completely ignore the subject of needs, on the grounds that it has already had more than its fair share of the philosophical limelight, and, on the other, propose that the educational importance of children's wants (or, more precisely, of the fact that children have wants) need not depend upon 'child-centred' or 'instrumental/motivational' considerations, but can be demonstrated by exposing the various logical connections which exist between wants and reasons, and which are particularly relevant to the concerns of *moral* education.

WANTS AND REASONS

To want something, I must see it under some attractive aspect and accordingly feel some inclination towards achieving, possessing or pursuing it. The attractiveness of what is wanted may be characterized in a wide variety of ways. I may want X because of what I see as its intrinsic attractions (e.g. I may want to garden rather than take the dog for a walk because I simply get more enjoyment from gardening); or I may want X because of its instrumental value in helping me to achieve a further attractive goal (e.g. I may want to garden rather than decorate the house in order that I may be able to enjoy fresh vegetables next year); or I may want X despite its *unattractive* qualities, because it represents the lesser of two evils (e.g. I may want to garden rather than stay indoors and help with the washing-up because I dislike washing-up even more than I dislike gardening). It is possible then for me to want anything which I can see *in some way* as attractive or relatively unattractive.

But not everything that I see as attractive do I necessarily want. I may meet an attractive woman at a party, or see an attractive picture on the wall, or hear an attractive tune on the radio, without wanting to do anything about any of them. They all appeal to me in some respect, but these qualities may not provide me with reasons which incline me to pursue what I see as attractive. There may be other reasons why I have no inclination to cultivate the woman's company, or make an offer for the picture, or try to remember the tune. I cannot be said, then, to want X if its attractions do not furnish me with some goals or ambitions. 'The primitive sign of wanting', as Anscombe puts it, 'is trying to get.'[2]

It follows from this that there must exist important logical connections between wants and reasons. There will always be reasons to explain why I want X, referring to that description of X which picks out the particular aspect of attractiveness under which I see it and which inclines me to pursue it (e.g. I may want a cottage in the country because I see it as offering peace and seclusion, which attract me and incline me to seek them). The fact that the same object or activity can be seen under many *different* aspects is the reason why we do not all have the same wants (e.g. others may see a country cottage not as a peaceful retreat but as a bad investment or a social backwater). Such characterizations provide both *the* reason why I want (or do not want) X and also *my* reason for wanting (or not wanting) X. My reason may, of course, be a bad reason (e.g. I may find that the attractions of a country cottage soon become outweighed for me by other aspects which I had not properly considered), but it still supplies the motive which explains retrospectively why I acted, or prospectively why I shall act, in a certain way.

It can, in fact, be argued that *only* wants can provide such reasons for action. Gauthier, for example, suggests that only a person's actual objective can provide a reason for acting, and that objectives are determined by the objects of our wants: 'Unless a consideration is capable of moving some person directly to deliberate action – unless it is an object of his wants – it cannot serve anyone as a genuine reason for acting'.[3]

The notion of a 'genuine reason for acting' is ambiguous, however, as it can refer either to a consideration which actually *motivates* me to do X, or to one which I consider *justifies* or *requires* my doing X. Our wants may well provide the only 'genuine reasons for action' in the first sense, but there seem also to be justificatory and obligatory considerations in the second sense, which we may acknowledge as reasons for acting in a certain way but which can *conflict* with our wants. Moral temptation consists of precisely such a conflict. Edgley underlines this point when he comments:

> There are, I think, . . . reasons of a sort such that their being some particular person's reasons for doing something does not imply that he wants to do that thing. Moral reasons seem to me to be of this kind.[4]

This does not mean, of course, that moral reasons must always and necessarily conflict with our wants. The fact that we may regard a set of considerations as constituting reasons which morally justify or require a certain action need not prevent us from also wanting to perform that action. If I think that there are moral reasons why I ought to visit a relative in hospital, I may well also want to visit him; I may see the action under various aspects of attractiveness which incline me to do what I believe I morally ought to do (e.g. I may enjoy his company, or be upset at the thought of him being lonely; or I may gain satisfaction from the prospect of doing what I conceive to be my duty *because* it is my duty). To quote Edgley again:

> It may, of course, be the case that if someone's reasons for doing something are moral reasons he also, as a matter of act, wants to do that thing and perhaps wants to do it *because* he thinks he morally ought to do it . . .[5] (Author's italics)

'Reasons for action' in moral contexts, then, reveal clearly the ambiguity noted above, for they may refer, on the one hand, to justificatory considerations which provide the backing for judgments about what one ought to do or, on the other, to motivational considerations which influence whether or not one actually does what one believes one ought to do. Wants appear to be related necessarily to motivational considerations, but only contingently to justificatory ones; we may not want (or not want strongly enough) to do what we believe we morally ought to do, if certain motivational considerations in a particular situation outweigh for us the justificatory ones, and we are then said to be guilty of moral weakness, which Kenny describes as 'a particular case of the problem of conflicting wants', for:

> When a man says that he ought to do something, he can always be asked 'Under pain of what ought you to do it?' and the answer may be 'Under pain of injustice, or unkindness, or folly', for example; and if he fails to do what he ought to do, this means that for the time being he wants something else more than he wants not to be unjust, or unkind, or foolish.[6]

This interpretation of moral weakness in terms of *conflicting* wants is not wholly satisfactory, for the distinction which has been drawn between justificatory and motivational considerations suggests that it is quite possible not to want *at all* to do what one believes one morally ought to do, in which case there would be no opposing want to create a conflict. Kenny's emphasis upon the role played by wants in cases of moral weakness is suggestive, however, in light of the logical connections between wants and reasons for action which have so far been outlined. If moral weakness involves wanting to do something else more than to do what one feels one ought to do, it follows that one way of countering moral weakness (and perhaps the only way) would be for the motivational scales to be tipped in the other direction, so that one comes to want to do what one feels one ought to do more than to do anything else.

IMPLICATIONS FOR CHILDREN'S WANTS

The logical connections between wants and various types of reason which have been briefly explored in the first section make children's wants philosophically much more interesting and educationally much more significant for rational and moral development than is usually allowed. In general terms it is difficult to see how a young child could start to grasp the idea of there being a *reason* for *acting* in a particular way other than through the medium of his wants, for wants serve as the paradigm example of how judgment and action can be rationally linked: one does X because one sees it in some way as attractive and is *for that reason* inclined to do something about it. As Peters points out:

> . . . 'wants' emerge from 'wishes' when children begin to grasp that means can be taken to bring about or avoid . . . pleasurable or painful conditions. And with the emergence of 'wants' the notion of 'reasons' emerges as well. For a 'reason for action' is that end, for the sake of attaining or avoiding which, means can be devised.[7]

This general point yields a number of more specific implications, five of which will now be considered.

1. If we are concerned in moral education with children's *actions* as well as with their levels of reasoning and judgment, and if we wish children to act for reasons which they can see *as* reasons, then we will have to take some account of what children want.

Kohlberg's characterization of the lower levels of moral development is of interest in this respect, for those considerations which a child acknowledges as constituting good reasons at a particular stage will presumably reflect the general class of wants which is dominant at that stage. (The reasons which Kohlberg has attempted to plot seem to refer to both justificatory and motivational factors; he speaks, for example, of 'the "motivational" aspect of morality [as] defined by the motive mentioned by the subject in justifying moral action'.[8]) So a child's reason for thinking it right to do something will be derived at Stage I from his wanting to avoid punishment, at Stage II from his wanting to gain rewards and physical satisfaction, and at Stage III from his wanting to gain social approval.

Despite Kohlberg's preoccupation with moral judgment rather than moral action, which will be explored further in Section Three, it still follows from his account that if a child is to be encouraged at whatever stage he is now at to do what he thinks is right *because* he thinks it is right, one can only rely on those considerations which he sees here and now as both justificatory and motivational, and which will in turn depend upon that class of wants which is at present most influential. There will be no point in urging a young child to share his toys by appealing to Stage III considerations of social approval (e.g. 'Your friends won't like you if you're selfish!') if he sees no attraction at that time in the gaining of such approval because his wants and reasons are orientated towards Stage I considerations of punishment-avoidance.

2. Similarly, if cases in which justificatory and motivational considerations conflict and in which a child is tempted to act other than as he believes he ought (i.e. cases of 'moral weakness') are explicable in terms of the agent failing to do what he believes he ought (X) because he wants to do something else more (Y), as Kenny suggests, then the task of moral education in such cases must be somehow to reverse the respective motivational attractions of X and Y in order that the child may come to want to do X more than Y and so do X rather than Y. One method which might be used here would be to suggest other descriptions and interpretations of the situation, thus drawing the child's attention to other features and factors within it which increase for him the attractiveness or lessen the unattractiveness of doing X, or lessen

the attractiveness or increase the unattractiveness of doing Y, so that the child for those reasons becomes more inclined to do X.

The child's *present* level of wants will again be crucial here. For example, a child who is tempted to cheat in a test and who is at Stage III of Kohlberg's developmental sequence may not have seen the situation as one in which his popularity and reputation within the class will suffer if his cheating is detected, and if this factor which will carry particular weight with him at this stage is emphasized, he may see the action of cheating under a new and less attractive aspect and accordingly not want to cheat. Equally, to underline the prospect of punishment to a child at Stage I, or of reward and physical satisfaction to a child at Stage II, would be, if Kohlberg is correct, to characterize the situation in terms of those reasons to which the child attributes most validity at that respective stage.

One obvious objection to the line of argument developed in (1) and (2) is that what children may happen to want at any particular time need possess no moral value and is therefore irrelevant to the business of moral education. How can a child learn what is right merely by consulting his wants or by being helped to reinterpret situations in the light of those wants? Such procedures can surely produce only a self-satisfied egoist.

The suggestions in (1) and (2), however, are not claiming that wants can provide or justify the content of children's moral *judgments*. As was pointed out in the first section, inclination and obligation often conflict, and we do not solve a moral problem (morally, at least) by deciding what we most want; deciding what one ought to do and what constitutes a justificatory consideration is only contingently related to what one wants. What is being claimed in (1) and (2) is that if one necessary, though by no means sufficient, aim of moral education is to encourage rational behaviour (i.e. doing X rather than Y for reasons which one accepts as good reasons), then it must take account of what children see as good reasons (in the motivational as well as the justificatory sense) for doing X rather than Y and of the wants which lie behind those reasons; a suggested alternative interpretation of a situation, for instance, must strike some chords with a child's present level of wants if he is both to *act* upon that interpretation and to regard it as providing a good reason for so acting.

Merely to utilize children's existing wants, however, as outlined in (1) and (2) clearly suffers from severe limitations as a means of moral education, and may even lead a teacher or parent to have to appeal to motivational considerations which he thinks are morally objectionable. Children's wants are not static entities, and it is at least as important for moral education to concentrate on their future modification as on their present utilization. The remaining three implications will deal with this aspect.

3. If we wish to try to *accelerate* children's moral and rational development, one important task will be to encourage examination and discussion of their wants. By exposing the interconnections between a child's wants and his reasons, a different and perhaps more constructive view of conflict situations may result. For example, a child who wants to be bought an expensive toy which his parents cannot afford might, after talking and reflecting about why he wanted it, realize that what he really sees as attractive is not the actual possession of the toy but the increased status he thinks the toy will give him when playing with his friends. The reasons why he sees *that* as attractive could in turn be discussed, and other ways of gaining his friends' approval explored. The parents could also distinguish between their wanting the child to enjoy playing with his friends and their wanting, for financial reasons, not to spend so much money on a toy. Such a situation could in this way come to be seen by the child not as one in which one simply 'has' wants which are arbitrarily either frustrated or gratified, but one in which conflicting wants can sometimes be resolved if they are redescribed and perhaps modified as a result of an examination of their rational basis.

4. Another way in which children's wants may be modified is by exposure to the prescriptive and persuasive functions of language. This also explains to some extent how children come to develop and formulate wants in the first place. To accept that certain actions count as being 'kind', 'unkind', 'fair', 'unfair', 'polite', 'rude', 'helpful', 'naughty', etc., or as 'telling lies', 'breaking promises', 'stealing', 'cheating', 'bullying', etc., is to adopt an evaluative stance towards those actions, which is delineated by whichever interpretative concepts are used. One of the reasons, then, why young children come to see certain things as attractive

or unattractive may well be that these are presented to them, apparently descriptively, in language which carries overtones of approval and disapproval, of recommendation and prohibition; and one of the reasons why we continue to hold reasonably consistent and stable values may well be that we have adopted from early childhood a linguistic framework of interpretation which crystallizes our evaluative attitudes and so helps to keep them constant. If a child has been brought up, for example, to think of policemen as heroic guardians of law and order and friendly servants of the public (as a result of the language to which he is exposed in parental teaching, stories and books), he will be in possession of a set of evaluative concepts which will incline him, other things being equal, in favour of respecting and liking the police and wanting to help them, rather than of despising and disliking them and wanting to impede them. It will need a drastic disillusionment and a consequent reversal of motivational weightings for him later to come to see policemen as 'fascist pigs'.

A child's concepts, values and wants, then, are closely interconnected. Moral language can be influential in the early development of wants, and it is interesting to speculate how close this procedure of exposing young children to prescriptive language in a descriptive guise comes to a form of indoctrination, if crystallized evaluative attitudes in fact result. At a later stage, moral language can also serve to modify children's wants by presenting to them alternative commentaries on and interpretations of situations which they encounter. Again, if these commentaries and interpretations are to produce not merely revised judgments but also action based on those judgments, they will have to strike some motivational chords with the child's existing wants and values. A major difficulty here will be how to bridge the gap between a self-interested and an altruistic perspective in such a way that the child comes to want to further the interests of others.

5. Other people's wants constitute an important (some would say the only) consideration in the forming of moral judgments and decisions. Thus Gauthier, for example, extends his thesis that only wants can provide reasons for action by arguing that in *moral* reasoning it is *other people's* wants that provide the reasons for action.[9] Again, however, the distinction between justificatory and motivational considerations must be drawn, for it is quite possible

to judge that another person's wants justify or require one's acting in a certain way but to want *not* to act in that way. Another concern of moral education, then, must be to bring the child to see other people's wants as motivational as well as justificatory considerations in deciding what to do. One obvious way of attempting this would be to establish a link between the child's wants and the wants of another person, so that the child comes to want the other's wants to be satisfied. This will in turn require the preconditions that:

(a) the child has some self-conscious awareness of what it is to want something himself, for he can otherwise have no conception of what it is for someone else to have wants,

(b) there be some affective and affectionate relationship between the child and the other person whose wants furnish the child with his *first* experience of an altruistic reason for action (i.e. he must want the other person to be happy rather than sad). It is difficult to see how altruistic considerations can initially be recognized by a child as reasons for acting to further the interests of another, unless he can 'identify' to some extent with those interests and want them to be furthered – though later he may be able to generalize such wants and detach them from the limitations of purely personal affection.

These five implications, which have been briefly outlined, suggest that children's wants, by virtue of their logical connections with reasons, cannot be regarded as educationally irrelevant. The emphasis throughout, however, has been upon *moral* education and the role played by children's wants in determining their reasons for *action*; but the alleged irrelevance of children's wants is also often maintained on more general educational grounds (i.e. that children need to learn and be taught about things which they do not necessarily want to know about, and that what they do want to know about may be educationally trivial). To examine the possible significance of children's wants in this wider context would require much more detailed treatment, but in conclusion I offer the following speculation on the relationship between children's wants and reasons in the moral and the intellectual spheres.

I have tried to argue that children's wants cannot be ignored in moral education because of their various connections with reasons for acting (i.e. with *practical* reason), and in particular because they are the medium by which children come to see facts as *factors*, bearing upon the question of whether to *do* X or Y. But where the development of *theoretical* reason is concerned it is equally necessary to come to see facts as *factors*, bearing in this case upon the question of whether to *believe* X or Y. The seeing of a fact as a factor, then, deriving normative force from its consequent status as a reason,[10] appears to be a common feature in the development of both practical and theoretical reason, and it might further be argued that the more direct motivational force exercised by a practical reason, as a result of its close association with wanting, suggests some logical or psychological priority over the less tangible force exercised by a theoretical reason; or, in other words, a child may be able to arrive at the notion of there being good reasons for believing that X rather than Y is the case only *after* having grasped that there are good reasons (deriving from his wants) for doing X rather than Y. If there is anything in this speculation, the educational importance of children's wants would be further extended, for they might then be said, in a sense, to form the basis of rationality by providing the foundations for the development of theoretical reasons for holding particular beliefs as well as of practical and moral reasons for performing particular actions.

NOTES AND REFERENCES

I am particularly indebted to Charles Clark for his detailed comments on an earlier draft of this chapter.

(1)   See, e.g. Hirst, P. H. and Peters, R. S. (1970) *The Logic of Education* (London: Routledge & Kegan Paul), chapter 2, and Dearden, R. F. (1972) ' "Needs" in education' in Dearden, R. F., Hirst, P. H. and Peters, R. S. (eds) *Education and the Development of Reason*, part 1 (London: Routledge & Kegan Paul).
(2)   Anscombe, G. E. M. (1957) *Intention* (Oxford: Basil Blackwell), p. 75.
(3)   Gauthier, D. P. (1963) *Practical Reasoning* (Oxford: Clarendon), p. 94.
(4)   Edgley, R. (1969) *Reason in Theory and Practice* (London: Hutchinson), p. 162.
(5)   Ibid.

(6)   Kenny, A. (1975) *Will, Freedom and Power* (Oxford: Basil Blackwell), p. 106.

(7)   Peters, R. S. (1966) *Ethics and Education* (London: Allen & Unwin), pp. 149–50.

(8)   Kohlberg, L. The development of children's orientations toward a moral order, *Vita Humana* **6** (1/2), 13.

(9)   *Op. cit.*, chapter VI.

(10) See, e.g. Edgley, *op. cit., passim.*

FURTHER QUESTIONS FOR CONSIDERATION

(1)   How can we find out what children *do* want?

(2)   What other methods might be tried to *modify* children's wants? Could there be moral objections to some methods of modification?

(3)   If different children in the same class have different wants and exhibit different *levels* of wants, what are the practical implications for the teacher?

(4)   Should teachers pay more attention to the prescriptive and persuasive features of the language they use with children?

(5)   How can children be encouraged to take other people's wants into account?

(6)   Can a child learn about X if he or she does not want to know about X?

Chapter 3

Educational Standards and Priorities

Recent debates about standards in education have been conducted with a passion and ferocity that have tended to obscure rather than clarify the issues at stake. Probably this is because many of the antagonists have felt that the issues are already perfectly clear-cut: educational standards are either rising, remaining constant, or falling, so all we have to do is find out empirically (or merely proclaim on the basis of intuition) which alternative is the correct one and what can be done to remedy the situation, if it is thought to need remedying.

This sort of assumption, which is implicit in much of the recent controversy, either ignores or grossly oversimplifies two central sets of questions which must be asked in any comprehensive discussion of educational standards, namely,

(a) *conceptual* questions about what is meant by 'educational standards', and

(b) *methodological* questions about how such standards can be measured and evaluated.

In this chapter we shall look principally at the first set of questions with the intention not of providing a definitive answer as to whether educational standards are in fact rising or falling, but rather of exploring what *prior* questions have to be asked before any such answer could be attempted. The latter part of the chapter will examine possible explanations of failures to achieve educational standards which have been set.

WHAT ARE EDUCATIONAL STANDARDS?

Standards, in education and elsewhere, refer to levels of achievement or expectation against which people and objects can be assessed. They thus indicate, on the one hand, the *values and priorities* which explain why certain levels rather than others are established (e.g. why one of the demands of the old 11+ examination was a high degree of proficiency in arithmetical computation) and, on the other hand, the existence of procedures which enable us to *measure and evaluate* on the basis of those levels (e.g. in the case of the 11+ again, a method of setting particular questions and marking them in particular ways which made it possible to measure the children's achievement).

This very generalized account of standards, however, does not take us very far, and in fact re-emphasizes the need to sort out the different kinds of question that have to be asked about educational standards. What sort of values and priorities lie behind the establishment of various educational standards, for example? Do standards refer primarily to achievements or expectations? How do we establish the levels against which children are to be measured? What exactly has to be compared with what before we can say that standards are rising or falling?

Let us start to clear the ground a little by considering some of the conceptual questions concerning standards. How is the concept actually used in the educational context? What different jobs does it have to perform and what different meanings and usages does it bear? What kinds of confusion can the ambiguity (if any) of the term create?

Firstly, and most obviously, 'standards' is not merely a descriptive term; it carries with it overtones of value, and these can take different forms:

(a) As has already been mentioned, standards reflect the values and priorities which lead to the establishment of certain levels and norms rather than others.

(b) The levels and norms themselves may be concerned with questions of value, including moral value, as well as questions of fact. For example, although recent debate about educational standards has usually been concentrated upon standards of skill, competence and intellectual attainment (e.g. are ten-year-olds better at reading now than they were twenty years ago?), concern has also been expressed about other sorts of standard – standards of behaviour, of discipline, of responsibility, of respect, of politeness, of dress, etc. (e.g. are ten-year-olds better behaved now than they were twenty years ago?). In the case of these latter standards, to decide what *constitutes* a rise or fall in them requires the making of a value judgment, perhaps an uncontroversial one but nevertheless a judgment which involves the holding of particular beliefs and the adoption of a particular moral stance (e.g. that standards of behaviour are falling if more ten-year-olds now are committing acts of vandalism, because vandalism is a bad thing).

(c) Even when we are talking about apparently non-moral standards in education (of skill, attainment, etc.), to describe a change in those standards as a 'rise' or a 'fall' carries with it some value-laden overtones of approval or disapproval. If, for example, I describe a change in children's abilities to know their tables as a fall in educational standards, there is a strong implication that I believe it to be a good thing for children to know their tables.

So questions about educational standards are not straightforward empirical questions of fact, and they cannot be discussed without reference being made, implicitly or explicitly, to questions of value. The second conceptual point which needs to be made, however, highlights a more direct source of confusion: the term 'educational standard' is radically ambiguous, as it can be used in several different senses:

(1) It can refer to a particular method of organizing an educational system, whereby children are classified according to the level of attainment they have reached and have their school career structured by a progression through a series of 'standards' or 'grades'. The historical connotations of this sense of 'standard' remove it to some extent from the central arena of the current debate, though it can at times be detected in arguments to the effect that too much concern for standards in schools will lead to 'standardization' and a consequent lack of flexibility and individualized teaching. The Plowden Report illustrated this view well:

We have considered whether we can lay down standards that should
be achieved by the end of the primary school, but considered that
it is not possible to describe a standard of attainment that should
be reached by all or most children. Any set standard would seriously limit the bright child and be impossibly high for the dull.
What could be achieved in one school might be impossible in another.[1]

This passage, apart from exemplifying how the orthodoxy of
one decade can become the heresy of another, demonstrates clearly the conceptual murkiness of the notion of 'standards'. Standards are here described as 'set', which creates further ambiguity.
All standards must of course be 'set' in the sense of being established, decided upon or laid down, because that is part of what
is meant by a standard. But 'set' can also mean rigid, fixed,
unalterable, and it seems to be this sense that the Plowden Report
is leaning upon when it goes on to talk about standards seriously
limiting bright children and being impossibly high for the dull.
Standards have here been *defined* as a 'set', rigid, system of standardization which will necessarily determine the organization of
the school, its curriculum and its teaching methods.

(2) Standards need not, of course, be interpreted in Plowden's
sense of organizational standardization. More commonly the term
is used simply to describe levels of attainment and competence
which are in fact being reached, and these levels need carry no
overtones of rigid standardization nor imply any particular organizational structure. Plowden's concluding revelation – 'What could
be achieved in one school might be impossible in another' – is no
argument against the use of standards in this more normal sense
of the term. Indeed there cannot really *be* an argument 'against'
standards in this sense, for all schools *must* have these sorts of
standard, even if their actual achievements are very low. The only
possible argument would be that it was undesirable to find out
and/or publicize what the standards of achievement actually were
in certain schools (perhaps because the results would be too discouraging), but that is an argument against the collection and/or
dissemination of information, not against 'having standards'.

This descriptive use of 'standards' then is not in itself value-
laden to the extent that other uses are: the bald statement 'The
standards of school X are A, B, C, . . .' appears in this sense to
be a simple report of the facts. Yet even here implications of

value-assumptions are lurking close at hand. Which achievements, for example, are being picked out as representative of the school's standards? Presumably the achievement of, say, linguistic and mathematical competence is more often taken as an indication of the school's standards than the speed at which the footballs are blown up or the amount of fidgeting during Assembly. But this selection involves the making of value-judgments, and though these may be relatively uncontroversial ones, as in the extreme example just given, it is not difficult to imagine cases where the characterization of what a school's standards of achievement actually were could raise serious problems because of the different priorities assigned to different values (e.g. the value of a low truancy rate versus that of a low 'A' level failure rate versus that of an unbeaten school football team). Not even in the Head Teacher's report on Speech Day can *everything* that is done in a school be described, so any account of a school's standards of achievement must be selective and thereby supportive of certain values and priorities rather than others.

(3) Standards may also be interpreted in a third sense, often confused with the second, which involves a much more obvious and straightforward expression of values. In this sense, standards refer not to levels of attainment which *have* actually been reached, but to levels which it is hoped, expected or desired *will* or *should* be reached. To describe a school's standards in this third sense, then, is to specify not its achievements but its aims, goals, objectives and aspirations, and this seems to be, in part at least, the kind of standard to which Plowden was objecting in denying the possibility of describing 'a standard of attainment that should be reached by all or most children'.

Why this should be thought to be impossible, however, is not at all clear. Do not schools and individual teachers *have* to 'have standards' in this sense if they are to operate purposefully and rationally? Such standards may not be explicitly declared, but they are surely implicit in virtually everything that a teacher or group of teachers tries to do within a school. How can one set about teaching an infant to do his shoe laces up or a 6th former to appreciate a novel without having *some* idea of the level of skill or understanding that one is hoping the learner will achieve? Without this kind of preconception, what goes on within a school must be wholly random and aimless, and it is difficult to see how such activities could count as 'teaching' or as 'education'. Of course, a teacher's or a school's expectations and hopes may not always (or even often) be fulfilled, and they may have to be modified if found to be unrealistic, but that again is no argument against 'having standards' in this sense. One has to have a target to aim at before one can tell what chance one has of hitting it.

Whereas standards in sense (b) tend to be those of the learner (i.e. what he achieves), standards in sense (c) tend to be those of the teacher or examiner (i.e. what he expects to be achieved or believes ought to be achieved) – though, of course, it is quite possible also to talk of teachers' achievements and children's expectations. The distinction between (b) and (c) is an important one, however, which can lead to confusion if ignored. A rise or a fall, for example, in 'achieved' standards implies no necessary, corresponding rise or fall in 'expected' standards, and vice versa. A record of progressively deteriorating examination results does not necessarily mean that a school is setting its sights lower and lower; indeed its standards of expectation may be rising, while its standards of achievement are falling. Similarly, it does not follow that if a school lowers its standards of expectation, its standards of achievement will necessarily fall; a modification of unrealistic demands could increase pupils' confidence and improve their performance.

The ambiguity of the term 'educational standards', therefore, means that some exploration of its different uses is essential before any claims about rising or falling standards can be considered and before any useful discussion can get off the ground. Unless the distinction between 'achieved' and 'expected' standards is recognized, for example, any generalizations about a school's standards are likely to be radically confused.

WHY ARE EDUCATIONAL STANDARDS NOT ALWAYS ACHIEVED?

The ambiguity noted above highlights another aspect of the central problem with which this book is concerned. It appears to be an unfortunate fact of human existence that we must always allow for the possibility of a gap opening up between our aspirations and our practice in all fields of our endeavours, and education is no exception to this. What teachers, parents, administrators, politicians – and indeed pupils – judge and believe to be desirable goals may often not in fact be attained, and consequently the 'achieved' standards of a school or a whole educational system may fail to correspond to the 'expected' standards.

No one simple explanation of such failures can, of course, be given, as they will occur in a variety of complex educational, social and political contexts. Yet some general pointers can be gained by reflecting upon the wider judgment/action problem and the possible reasons why beliefs are not always translated into behaviour.

One recurring theme of this book is the all-important role played by our wants in influencing how we behave. When we apparently fail to act as we believe we ought and thus to live up to our avowed standards, one possible explanation is that we, in fact, want to do something else more, though we are reluctant to admit it: we believe that we ought to do X, but in fact want to do Y more than X, and so do Y, though still maintaining that X ought to be done because we do not wish openly to acknowledge the attractions of Y. This explanation will be examined in more detail in the following chapter, but it is worth considering it briefly at this point to see if it makes any sense in relation to educational standards and failures associated with them.

Let us take as a simple test case the example given in the Introduction of Tony, a student teacher on teaching practice, who fails to achieve certain standards of classroom management and effective teaching by ignoring basic techniques of control. Let us suppose that Tony knows what he ought to do to avoid the problem developing and that he sincerely believes that his teaching ought to come up to the highest standards of which he is capable. How, then, can his failure be accounted for, assuming that he is physically and mentally able to take the appropriate action? Only, I suggest, by attempting to identify those things which Tony on that occasion and in that situation really wants most. He might, for example, fail to tackle the potential trouble-makers because he most of all wants to avoid conflict and the implied threat to his authority, or to be popular, or to safeguard his blood pressure, or to talk only to those pupils with whom he feels some intellectual rapport. But it would be difficult for him to acknowledge openly, or even to himself, that these are his real, though less praiseworthy, priorities in that situation, and so the incident comes to be interpreted misleadingly (by an observer or by Tony himself) as an example of 'weakness' or of 'low standards' or of 'failing to put theory into practice'. Such interpretations are unhelpful as well as misleading, because their likely effect will be merely to increase Tony's feelings of guilt and inadequacy, which will probably be counter-productive; whereas the suggested analysis of the incident in terms of wants could encourage Tony to examine and reflect critically upon his real priorities and the assumptions underlying them, and thereby, perhaps, to modify and reformulate them.

Can this analysis be extended beyond simple individual examples and applied to the broader problem of failure to achieve 'expected' educational standards? What can be said in general terms about the teacher or the department or the school or the local authority or the educational system which fails to attain those goals which are judged to be desirable? Many factors may, of course, contribute to such failures, and this is not the place for a full-scale review, but the teaching practice example does suggest one important dimension to these problems which is often ignored in the current climate of opinion, where all educational difficulties and failures tend to be attributed indiscriminately to a 'lack of resources'.

In the above example it was suggested that Tony failed to sort out his priorities and formulate clearly what he most wanted to achieve. A similar failure can beset experienced teachers, groups of teachers and educational institutions. If one explicitly sets X, Y and Z as one's desired educational goals or standards, but finds that in pursuing X, Y, Z one is faced with other less explicit demands and expectations, A, B, C, which one perhaps wants to satisfy even more than X, Y, Z, it becomes less likely that X, Y, Z will be achieved.

This again is most easily demonstrated from the viewpoint of an individual teacher, who may set or accept standards of attainment which he believes he ought to be able to attain with his pupils, but then finds that other priorities which (for various reasons) he wants to satisfy, possibly of a pastoral or administrative kind, are taking up so much of his time and energy that he is failing to reach his declared goal. Indeed, this predicament can hardly be avoided by any teacher who finds time to dip into the latest textbook on 'The Role of the Teacher', and is confronted with the usual formidable list of things that teachers allegedly ought to be doing *in addition to* 'mere teaching'.

A similar conflict can equally well be experienced by a subject department, or a whole school or education authority. As in the case of Tony, the probable result will be an individual or generalized feeling of guilt, inadequacy and 'weakness', which tends to mask what is really happening: priorities are becoming confused because the initial statement of aims and expected standards is unrealistic in not making allowance for other, often undeclared, demands and wants.

If there is anything in the above hypothesis, it would follow that current concern over the problem of 'teacher stress' is not misplaced. Perhaps such 'stress' should not be simplistically interpreted merely as teachers 'trying to do too much', but rather as the symptom of much more fundamental educational problems arising from the setting and attainment (or non-attainment) of educational standards and the complex ways in which teachers' beliefs about their aims are related to their actual performance and to their own assessments of that performance.[2]

NOTES AND REFERENCES

(1)   Plowden Report (1967) *Children and their Primary Schools*, vol. 1 (London: HMSO), para. 551.
(2)   Part of this chapter originally appeared in *Values and Evaluation in Education* (Harper & Row, 1980), which I co-edited with Jack Wrigley. I wish to thank my co-editor and colleagues at the University of Reading School of Education who contributed to the book for their helpful comments on some of the original material.

FURTHER QUESTIONS FOR CONSIDERATION

(1)   Do you agree with the Plowden Report that 'any set standard would seriously limit the bright child'?
(2)   Should standards of achievement in particular schools ever be kept confidential?
(3)   Can teaching or learning go on without reference to standards?
(4)   How exactly should a teacher or group of teachers set about the task of establishing priorities?

(5)   What problems are involved in deciding whether a goal is 'unrealistic'? How should teachers set their goals?

(6)   If a teacher reflects critically upon his or her wants and priorities and consequently modifies them, does this mean that standards have been lowered?

Section Two

Chapter 4

Judgment and Action in Moral Education

Although there has been a number of references to moral education in the previous section, Chapters 1–3 have in the main dealt with more general educational issues and have not confined their area of inquiry exclusively to the relationship between *moral* judgment and action. Nevertheless, morality probably provides the most obvious and dramatic context in which conflicts and inconsistencies occur between our judgments and actions, and the question then arises as to what function, if any, moral education can or should perform in this connection. To put it at its simplest, is it possible to teach children to behave in accordance with their moral beliefs and judgments? This is clearly an important question in view of the current concern for young people's standards of behaviour, in and out of school, although paradoxically moral education seems at present to be attracting less interest in educational circles than the more fashionable 'personal and social education'. However, it can be argued that there must necessarily be a central moral component in all programmes of 'personal and social education', for these will inevitably be aimed at particular 'personal and social' goals which are deemed to be *morally* desirable.[1]

The judgment/action issue can, in fact, be shown to have numerous implications for both moral education and moral development, and some of these will be analysed in some detail in this and the following section. This chapter will try to set the scene, first by drawing attention to some general, fundamental features of moral education and moral development, and secondly by focusing upon one specific problem within moral education.

The first task is to underline a few obvious but important points about why the philosophical issue of 'judgment and action' must lie at the very heart of moral education and development – indeed at the heart of morality itself. The nature of morality consists of a complex mixture and interaction of judgments and actions, of beliefs and behaviour. I am behaving morally when I act in accordance with certain judgments, reasons and intentions which lead me to believe that I *ought* to act in that way. It follows that we cannot look merely at a person's outward behaviour to determine whether or not he is acting morally. The same piece of outward behaviour (handing over some money, for example) can be interpreted in many different ways because of the many different reasons and intentions which may lie behind it. We cannot begin to judge whether the action of handing over some money on a particular occasion could be called 'moral', 'non-moral' or 'immoral', without knowing something of the agent's reasons and intentions – though, of course, philosophers are far from being agreed about precisely what *kind* of reasons and intentions are required for moral action.

Most philosophers and non-philosophers, however, probably would agree that, although having certain reasons and intentions of some kind is a *necessary* part of being a moral agent, this cannot be *sufficient* to constitute moral agency, for those intentions and motives must also lead one actually to perform the appropriate action. Morality is, by definition, a practical business, in that it is basically concerned with what ought to be done, and what it is right to do. Working out answers to moral problems and dilemmas in a purely theoretical way, as one solves a crossword clue, is not alone enough to qualify as 'being moral' if there is no consequent attempt made to act in accordance with one's conclusions.

So no adequate account of morality can be given *just* in terms of making particular kinds of judgment, or *just* in terms of performing particular kinds of action. Morality must refer to how a person both thinks and behaves. And if that is true of morality itself, it must also be true of moral education and moral development. No account of moral education or development, then, can be adequate if it concentrates exclusively either upon children's judgments and reasoning or upon their actions and behaviour.

Now this is where these apparently obvious points about the nature of morality start to assume some real practical importance, because many approaches to moral education and development fall into the trap of ignoring this complex balance between judgment and action and of overemphasizing one at the expense of the other.

There is, for example, one influential psychological tradition which has tried to study moral development predominantly in terms of children's moral *judgments*. Within this tradition, which goes back at least to Piaget's pioneering work in the 1930s, the level of thinking shown in a moral conflict situation, the cognitive complexity of the child's moral judgment and the type of reason given to justify a decision have been among the major factors thought most relevant in assessing moral development. Developmental psychologists, then, have tended to see moral development as concerned primarily with the form or structure of children's moral thinking, and characterized not so much by what the child actually does as by the reasons why he thinks he ought or ought not to do it. The classic expression of this view is to be found in the introduction to Piaget's highly influential book, *The Moral Judgment of the Child*, where he states:

> Readers will find in this book no direct analysis of child morality as it is practised in home and school life or in children's societies. It is the moral judgment that we propose to investigate, not moral behaviour or sentiments.[2]

Lawrence Kohlberg and his associates are, to some extent, the modern representatives of this tradition – though I am not suggesting that either Piaget or Kohlberg totally ignores moral action and behaviour. Both have some interesting things to say on that subject but, nevertheless, the main thrust of their work, and indeed their whole methodology, is directed towards an investigation of moral judgment and reasoning rather than moral actions and behaviour.

Now, this 'judgmental' approach to moral development has had an undoubted effect upon modern conceptions of moral education. Traditional notions of moral training or instruction, aimed at inculcating in children a particular code of moral conduct (e.g. telling the truth; respecting one's elders; playing one's hardest for the school), have largely been replaced by an emphasis upon furthering children's understanding of moral issues by teaching 'moral skills' and methods of moral reasoning – though moral education programmes in the British Isles have not gone quite so far as the Canadian Mackay Report on Moral Development, for example, which leaned heavily on Kohlberg's work for its theoretical backing and stated baldly: 'We equate character development with the development of the ability to reason morally'.[3]

In contrast to these 'judgmental' approaches, there are opposing traditions which seem to overemphasize behaviour at the expense of judgment – for example, the psychological, behaviourist tradition and its modern manifestation, behaviour modification. So we find B. F. Skinner, for example, maintaining that accounts of morality should avoid all reference to 'mentalistic phenomena' like beliefs and intentions, and to concepts of choice, responsibility and justice; a person acts morally not because he knows or feels that his behaviour is right, but because of the 'contingencies' which have 'shaped his behaviour'.[4]

Again, we can see this 'behavioural' approach to morality reflected in certain conceptions of moral education, or perhaps in this case moral training. The whole aim of the educational exercise on this view is that children should be taught or made to 'behave properly'. Levels of judgment and quality of reasoning are all very well, but it is what the child does that ultimately counts. New courses may be introduced in schools, aimed at getting children to discuss moral questions, but it is standards of behaviour (in and out of school) which signify the success or failure of moral teaching.

To summarize, then, this first very general and very obvious point, if we focus excessively or exclusively upon *either* judgment *or* action in our approach to moral education and moral development, we are distorting the very nature of morality, which consists of a complex interaction *between* judgment and action. Both judgmental and behavioural criteria must be satisfied before we can say that moral education has succeeded or that moral development has taken place.

This first point leads directly to the second. This concerns a specific, practical problem, which moral education often fails to tackle – the problem of moral weakness, of which we should all have plenty of practical experience in our daily lives – unless we are saints.

What has been said so far about judgment and action strongly implies the possibility of moral weakness. For example, the claim has been made that even if a child has learned skills which satisfy certain judgmental criteria for moral reasoning, this cannot be sufficient to demonstrate that he has been successfully morally educated, for he may fail to act upon the judgment which he has formed. There is, on the face of it, no reason to deny that a child (or adult) may at times judge that he ought to do X, perhaps revealing considerable moral maturity in arriving at this judgment, yet then deliberately fail to do X. Such a person could hardly claim to have acted morally or to have had an effective moral education.

The educational problem of moral weakness, then, is concerned with how to teach or encourage children to act upon their moral judgments, an issue on which I have written at some length elsewhere[5] and which I shall try to summarize as follows.

What exactly is happening when we fail to act upon our moral judgments, when we are guilty of moral weakness? Many different types of explanation are possible, and each explanation points to a particular kind of method for the moral *educator* to employ in trying to tackle the problem of moral weakness. There are, for example, a number of *causal* explanations, which suggest that we are at times overcome by overpowering emotions, desires or other irrational factors; we are simply not strong enough to withstand these pressures because either our will or our conscience is too weak. So moral education, according to this account, will aim to help children to control or repress their emotions, to build up a strong character and conscience, and to increase their will-power.

These causal, mechanistic explanations are not, in my view, convincing.[6] There is no reason to suppose that any distinct mental organ, called the 'will' or 'conscience', exists and can be identified, and we should not therefore assume the existence of such entities merely to explain why we at times fail to do what we believe we ought to do; one cannot explain that sort of phenomenon simply by inventing labels like 'weak will' to describe it.[7]

What is happening in so-called cases of 'moral weakness' is not a battle between our 'will' (whatever that might be) and our emotions, but rather a conflict or incompatibility between two different kinds of reason for action.

The notion of a 'reason for action' is in fact highly ambiguous, which can and does lead to a lot of confusion. Reasons can justify and they can motivate. These two functions are logically separate, though they may often combine in practice. If I believe that I ought to do X, I am acknowledging that there are good justificatory reasons for my doing X, which will be derivable from some more generalized principle. I may, for instance, believe that I ought to visit my aunt in hospital, because hospital patients generally like to be visited and cheered up, it may help my aunt to recover more quickly, and I would want to be visited if I were in her situation. So I am signifying my agreement with the principle that visiting relatives in hospital is in general a good thing, and am thereby acknowledging that there are good justificatory reasons for visiting my aunt; but I am not necessarily signifying any personal desire or inclination to visit her. Perhaps I do not have the time or the energy; perhaps I dislike my aunt intensely; or perhaps I dislike the atmosphere of hospitals even more intensely. I may, then, have no reason at all which motivates me to visit my aunt, as I would have if I were fond of her or if she were going to leave me all her money.

A crucial distinction, therefore, is being suggested between reasons which justify and reasons which motivate. This distinction offers us a general explanation for the phenomenon of moral weakness: a person may fail to do what he thinks he ought to do because he does not want to do what he thinks he ought to do (or wants to do something else more).

It might, however, be objected at this point that my proposed distinction (upon which the argument of this chapter ultimately depends) is in fact false, or at least too stark. Do not justificatory reasons always carry with them some motivational overtones? May not motivational reasons also provide a justification? Am I not ignoring the possibility of a person (a) being most strongly motivated by those considerations which he feels to be justificatory, or (b) maintaining that whatever he most wants is justified simply because he most wants it?

My reply to such objections would be, firstly, that of course we sometimes (perhaps often, and in some saintly cases even always) want to do what we think we ought to do because we believe there are good justificatory reasons for so acting. Inclination and obligation may often coincide in this way, but when they do it is still *two* logically separate kinds of consideration which are on these occasions overlapping. The possibility always remains of a conflict between justificatory and motivational reasons, and it is this conflict which in practice produces instances of moral weakness and indeed provides the whole business of morality with its unique and distinctive tensions. It is always possible and meaningful to ask the question, 'Why should I do what I morally ought to do?'[8] It follows, secondly, from this that the mere fact of wanting to do something cannot morally justify that action. Moral justifications reach beyond particular personal wants to general principles which by definition are of wider application than individual desires. If everything I want is thereby morally justified, moral justification loses all meaning and becomes a vacuous concept. The distinction between justificatory and motivational reasons must therefore be preserved, though in practice the relationship between the two will often be complex; it is, for example, quite possible to believe *that* X ought to be done and to *want* X to be done, but not to want *to do* X oneself.[9]

Can a more detailed picture be painted of this possible conflict between justificatory and motivational reasons? The morally weak person sincerely believes that there are good justificatory reasons why he ought to do X, yet there are also operative motivational reasons for not doing X. These latter reasons will derive from his wants, which lead him to see something else as more desirable than X in some way. What he is doing, then, in effect is to acknowledge explicitly the validity of the justificatory reasons which underlie his ought-judgment, without making explicit the motivational reasons which are, in fact, weighing more heavily with him at the time of his decision or action. So moral weakness appears to involve a particular kind of self-deception or intellectual dishonesty, in so far as the agent, in forming his ought-judgment, fails to spell out to himself (or to others) the motivational factors which are really influencing his course of action. Thus, my belief that I ought to visit my aunt in hospital is only part of my overall appraisal of the situation. The reasons which justify my visiting her are in practice outweighed by motivational factors such as my fear of hospitals; yet I make explicit only my ought-judgment and my justificatory reasons (which are morally respectable), and avoid reference to my inclinations and my motivational reasons (which are morally disreputable). In this way my apparently puzzling behaviour in not visiting my aunt as I believe

I ought comes to be attributed to my 'weakness', whereas the real explanation is that I want to avoid hospitals more than I want to visit my aunt.

At the heart of so-called 'moral weakness', then, is a refusal to admit and spell out what one really wants most, when expressing one's appraisal of a moral conflict situation. This happens because to make explicit one's overall appraisal would be to admit the greater priority one is assigning to non-moral than to moral considerations. By this means one can misleadingly attribute one's subsequent 'lapse' to overwhelming emotion or a weak will or a weak conscience, all of which appear to offer a partial excuse on the grounds that one did not really choose to behave as one did.

This interpretation of moral weakness explores only one dimension of the problem, but this is not the place for a more detailed analysis.[10] Even this single dimension, however, yields some interesting implications for moral education, to which we can now finally turn.

It could be objected at this point that the educational implications of my interpretation are in fact very limited. Even if, the argument might go, we can teach children to make more honest and open appraisals of their wants and motives, this is not necessarily going to overcome the problem of moral weakness and make it more likely that a child will act upon his moral judgments. He will simply have a fuller understanding and a more open acceptance of his reasons for acting as he does, so becoming a more self-aware egotist than he was before.

My reply to that objection would be that it is surely necessary as a first step to be aware of what one most wants before one can start to re-examine or consciously modify those wants. So any teaching methods which start by encouraging children to acknowledge and explore what their present wants and motives are may also be influential in leading them to make more considered appraisals of those wants and motives, and consequently perhaps to modify them. If my interpretation of moral weakness is valid, it follows that it can only be combated by modifying one's wants in some way and by making one's motivational reasons for action coincide with the justificatory ones.

What teaching methods might help to produce this kind of self-knowledge? Direct instruction seems unlikely to achieve very much, though there could be some value in introducing older children to some psychological and sociological theories of motivation. Group discussion also has certain built-in drawbacks, as it will inevitably take place within the context of group norms and expectations, which will establish what are acceptable, respectable priorities and values within the group; this could inhibit the individual child from acknowledging his own priorities, even to himself.

If self-deception and intellectual dishonesty are to be avoided, therefore, the moral educator will need to foster an atmosphere that is as free as possible from conventional constraints, where children do not feel vulnerable to moral censure. Mutual consideration and sympathetic understanding within the group will be prerequisites here. If a non-censorious ethos of this kind can be created, there should be more chance of a child acknowledging, examining and appraising his motivational reasons for action (e.g. why he prefers playing football with his friends to looking after his little sister), and consequently less danger of him merely saying what he thinks he is expected to say (e.g. 'I ought to look after my little sister more often'). Some of the recent approaches to personal, social and moral education, such as values clarification and active tutorial work, might be used for this purpose.[11]

The more traditional methods of moral exhortation and preaching seem likely to prove counterproductive if used to combat moral weakness, for they are designed to establish precisely the kind of censorious atmosphere in which the notion of moral weakness has its natural home. Such an atmosphere will encourage the explicit expression of justificatory reasons and will discourage the admission of motivational ones if they appear to be morally disreputable.

If moral education, then, is to take proper account of the problem of moral weakness, it must guard against the child setting his moral sights too high or having them set for him too high, initially at least. Unrealistic moral demands, whether self-imposed or externally imposed, can result only in failure, discouragement, and either cynicism or a guilt-ridden retreat to self-deception and the misleading excuse of a 'weak will'. This conclusion is perhaps best summed up in a passage by John Benson, which should give food for thought to moral educators as well as to moral philosophers.

I should welcome the recognition that the suppression of desires is sometimes just not worth the sweat and one would do better to adopt a principle which is easier to live with. Writers on ethics still tend to speak as though the task of the will is to beat the passions into submission in the interests of morality. There is also the task of exploring one's powers in order to discover what principles one can realistically commit oneself to. Weakness of will is sometimes what, in our zeal for self-castigation, we call the inevitable result of moral hubris.[12]

This notion of 'exploring one's powers in order to discover what principles one can realistically commit oneself to' could be said to offer a controversial definition of what moral education and development fundamentally consist of. Such a definition would of course need a lengthy investigation and defence if it were to be sustained; one obvious objection, for example, would concern the *level* of principles required to count as 'moral'. Moral principles presumably cannot be *too* easy to live with if the distinction between justificatory and motivational considerations is to be upheld. Nevertheless, Benson's account, which suggests some interesting links with some recent theological work on self-awareness and self-acceptance,[13] goes some way towards bridging the inevitable gap between judgment and action, which must, however, always remain a necessary component of morality itself and thereby a central concern of moral education.

NOTES AND REFERENCES

(1) For an elaboration of this argument, see Straughan, R. (1988) *Can We Teach Children to be Good? Basic Issues in Moral, Personal and Social Education*, new edition (Milton Keynes: Open University Press), pp. 23–6.
(2) Piaget, J. (1932) *The Moral Judgment of the Child* (London: Routledge), Foreword.
(3) Committee on Religious Education in the Public Schools of Ontario (1969) *Religious Information and Moral Development* (Toronto: Ontario Department of Education).
(4) Skinner, B. F. (1974) *About Behaviourism* (London: Cape), p. 193.
(5) Straughan, R. (1982) *I Ought to, But . . . : A Philosophical Approach to the Problem of Weakness of Will in Education* (Windsor: NFER-Nelson). Much of the original material for this chapter is drawn from this book.

(6)   Ibid., chapter 4.
(7)   See e.g. Hirst, P. H. (1974) *Moral Education in a Secular Society* (London: University of London Press), pp. 70–1.
(8)   See Frankena, W. K. (1958) 'Obligation and motivation' in Melden, A. I. (ed.) *Essays in Moral Philosophy* (Seattle and London: University of Washington Press), p. 47.
(9)   See Straughan, R. (1982) *op. cit.*, pp. 50–7.
(10)   See ibid., chapter 6.
(11)   See e.g. Raths, L., Harmin, M. and Simon, S. (1978) *Values and Teaching* (Columbus, OH: Charles Merrill); and Button, L. (1982) *Group Tutoring for the Form Teacher* (London: Hodder and Stoughton).
(12)   Benson, J. (1968) Oughts and wants, *Proceedings of the Aristotelian Society* **XLII**, 172.
(13)   See e.g. Williams, H. (1972) *True Resurrection* (London: Mitchell Beazley).

FURTHER QUESTIONS FOR CONSIDERATION

(1)   Should moral education concentrate on improving pupils' abilities to form moral judgments? How might this be done?

(2)   What do you think Piaget means by 'moral sentiments'? How are they related to judgments and behaviour?

(3)   What problems are raised if moral education is seen as a matter of 'shaping behaviour'?

(4)   Is it ever helpful to explain children's behaviour (or misbehaviour) in terms of a 'weak will' or a 'weak conscience'?

(5)   What problems might be involved in encouraging pupils to re-examine and modify their wants?

(6)   Should teachers encourage pupils to 'adopt a principle which is easier to live with'? What are the dangers of this approach?

(7)   Must moral, personal and social education ultimately be judged on how pupils actually behave?

Chapter 5

Hypothetical Moral Situations

In the previous chapter it was argued that morality is by definition a practical business, in that it is basically concerned with what ought to be done and what it is right to do. This presents problems for moral education, as it is clearly much easier for the teacher in the classroom to organize discussions about moral issues than practical programmes of moral activity. The researcher faces similar difficulties to those of the teacher. Both need somehow to create authentic moral situations or dilemmas for children to experience – the teacher in order to encourage discussion and decision-making on moral issues, the researcher in order to analyse responses and to assess moral development.

The way to achieve maximum authenticity would no doubt be to place children actually in situations of real moral conflict, e.g. by tempting them to cheat in a test or to steal school property. Such an approach has occasionally been attempted by researchers,[1] but the ethical and practical objections to it are so obvious that moral educationists have come to rely heavily both in teaching and in testing upon the use of *hypothetical* moral situations. These can be defined as situations which may be either fact or fiction, which can be described or portrayed to persons outside the situations, which appear to pose moral problems or dilemmas, and which allow subsequent questions to be asked in the form, 'What should the person in that situation have done?' or, more directly, 'What would *you* have done in that situation?' Examples of this approach are provided on the research side by the work of Kohlberg,[2] who has tried to plot children's levels of moral development by the use of hypothetical moral situations (for instance, should a man leave or stay at his civilian air-defence post after a heavy bombing raid that may have endangered his family?), and on the teaching side by the Schools Council Moral Education Project,[3] which bases virtually all of its *Lifeline* material upon hypothetical moral situations (for instance, a close friend of yours who has left school spends most of the day playing a guitar in his room; he collects Social Security, expects you to help him and says he has no intention of working; what do you do?).

Underlying this approach seems to be a basic assumption that there must be a straightforward and close connection between the student's response to a hypothetical situation and his response to a similar situation encountered in real life, or in other words that there must be a direct transfer from the moral judgment formed in a hypothetical situation to the decision made and the action performed in a real-life situation. So we find McPhail claiming of the *Lifeline* material, 'Without doubt work of this kind can produce improvements in behaviour as well as in attitude . . .' and again, 'The use of the "What would you have done?" series is intended to encourage in pupils . . . a willingness to act upon one's beliefs'.[4]

The purpose of this chapter will be to question these assumptions and to explore the possible limitations of the hypothetical moral situation approach by examining certain logical features of moral judgments in both hypothetical and non-hypothetical contexts. Some distinctions, however, must first be drawn between different types of hypothetical moral dilemma.

The type of dilemma frequently used by moral educationists involves a conflict of principles or obligations. In another Kohlberg situation, for example, where a husband can obtain a drug necessary for his sick wife's recovery only by stealing it, the principles of honesty and respect for property conflict with those of alleviating suffering and caring for one's family. But it is arguable whether this type of situation is empirically as common or logically as central a case of moral conflict as when the clash is between principle and inclination; e.g. I know that I *ought* to tell the policeman the truth about the speed at which I was driving, but I also know that it will get me into trouble and I do not *want* to get into trouble. Moral education has surely as much to do with the everyday problems of motivation and weak will which constantly face children as well as adults (e.g. should I own up and prevent the whole class being punished?) as with the moral conundrums of conflicting principles, so dear to moral philosophers. Yet it is the latter which tend to feature in hypothetical moral situations.

Conflicts of principle versus principle and of principle versus inclination must therefore be considered separately, while a further distinction can be made between 'first person' and 'third person' judgments, depending upon whether the question posed is in the form 'What would you do (or have done) in that situation?' (first person) or 'What should he (the subject of the story) do (or have done)?' (third person). Armed with these distinctions, we can now examine in turn the various types of hypothetical moral situation.

PRINCIPLE VERSUS INCLINATION SITUATIONS

The problem here is whether such a situation, like the policeman example, can qualify in any real sense as a 'moral' situation or as a 'moral' experience for the listener to whom it is presented hypothetically. What seems to be lacking in the hypothetical presentation is precisely that feature which would make the real-life situation a *moral* problem – immediacy. It is the immediacy of the inclination (not to get into trouble with the police) which I experience at first hand that *creates* the moral conflict; it is my own situational reasons, motives, wants and emotions which clash with the principle of truth-telling, and so face me with a moral decision to make. The actual motivational effect, though, of states of mind like fear, love, grief and awe cannot be properly appreciated secondhand. However many novels I have read or plays I have seen in which people fall in love or suffer bereavement, and however well I can describe the situation and feelings of those people, it will still be a completely new and different experience for me when I personally encounter love or bereavement for the first time. The psychological effect that these experiences will have on me cannot be rehearsed beforehand.[5]

Consequently it is impossible also to rehearse hypothetical principle versus inclination situations, because the inclination is not something that can be experienced secondhand. It will be the immediate situational factors (e.g. the policeman's manner; my particular fear of publicity at that time; the hangover I have from the night before) that help to decide whether principle or inclination wins. The use of this type of hypothetical situation, then, seems unable to contribute much to the testing or the developing of moral understanding, as the quality of immediacy which is a necessary and integral feature of moral situations must be absent, whether it is first or third person judgments that are being made.

The way in which these judgments are invited can also be a source of confusion and misinterpretation, whatever type of hypothetical situation is being presented. Questions which are put in the form, 'What would you do . . . ?' or 'What do you do . . . ?' are highly ambiguous as they could be taken to mean either 'What do you predict that your action (or reaction) would be . . . ?' or 'What decision do you think you ought to make . . . ?' and these are very different questions. The answer to the prediction question is descriptive, while the answer to the decision question is prescriptive, and the two may point in opposite directions; for instance, I may predict that I *shall* tell the policeman a lie, but decide that I *ought* to tell him the truth. Prediction and decision are separate activities, and they must be carefully distinguished when questions are asked about any type of hypothetical moral situation.

PRINCIPLE VERSUS PRINCIPLE SITUATIONS

Hypothetical situations involving a conflict of principles are also in a sense secondhand. The problem here though is not the impossibility of rehearsing the experience of a counter-inclination, but rather the nature of the relationship between a hypothetical and an actual (i.e. situational) moral decision. Is it inevitable that a principle which we accept as valid and overriding in a hypothetical situation must be considered as equally valid and overriding in a parallel, actual situation? In examining this question, the distinction between first and third person judgments must be applied.

Suppose that a child is presented with a hypothetical dilemma of conflicting principles described in the third person, as in the Kohlberg examples already quoted, and is asked, 'Should he have done that?' (e.g. the husband stealing the drug). The child is here being asked to form his own moral judgment about the decision and action of a third person, but it is debatable whether this kind of transference is possible in moral reasoning.

Winch, for instance, has used the hypothetical moral problem that is posed by the story of Billy Budd and Captain Vere to argue that if he (Winch) had been faced with Vere's dilemma of whether to enforce the military code or to follow his private conscience, he would have found it morally impossible under such circumstances to decide on the former and thus to condemn a man 'innocent before God'. But, the argument continues, it does not necessarily follow from this that Winch thinks that Vere acted wrongly; he did what was *for him* the right thing.[6]

Such an argument challenges the commonly held doctrine that all moral judgments are by nature universalizable, by claiming, in effect, that all moral situations are unique; even if two situations appear identical, they must be regarded as being dissimilar if each involves a different agent with a different moral disposition and perspective, and for whom there are different possibilities of moral interpretation. Hare, despite his allegiance to the universalizability doctrine, seems to reinforce this point when he claims, 'Since we cannot know everything about another actual person's concrete situation (including how it strikes him which may make all the difference) it is nearly always presumptuous to suppose that another person's situation is exactly like one we have ourselves been in or even like it in the relevant particulars'.[7]

One effect of this argument is to cast doubt upon the value of using hypothetical moral situations which involve a conflict of principles. How can anyone judge whether the husband was right to steal the drug and to place the value of life above the value of property, without knowing how he saw the situation and from which moral (or non-moral) perspective – without standing in the husband's moral shoes? The theft of the drug could be seen in an infinite number of different ways – for example, as a protest against profiteering chemists or against a callous God, as a symbol of unconditional love for the wife, or as a shrewd bid to restore to working efficiency the household's cook, washer-up and child-minder. To know which interpretation was correct would require a vast amount of detailed biographical and psychological information on the husband, and even given this it is still probably impossible to view a situation completely through another's eyes.

A further implication of the argument would be that if I am faced with this type of hypothetical moral problem, my judgment about what the husband ought to have done need bear no relation to what I judge that I ought to have done in that situation, because the fact that a different agent with a different perspective is involved makes it a different situation. If the interlocutor, however, tries to get over this problem by rephrasing his question in the form, 'What would you do if you were the husband?' he should be aware that his question is riddled with ambiguity. Firstly, is he asking a prediction question or a decision question, as distinguished above? And secondly, is he asking me to put myself into the place of a third person and to make the decision or prediction from that person's moral standpoint, or is he asking me to put myself personally into the situation described and to make the decision or prediction from my own moral standpoint? If he intends the former, there is a case for arguing that the task is impossible; if the latter, it is surely unnecessary and misleading to introduce the fiction of a third person at all.

These logical points about third person judgments suggest a further weakness in the hypothetical moral situation approach to moral education, as it is currently being used. The scanty amount of information that is normally provided means that the stories or events described can hardly qualify as 'situations' at all. They are more like cartoons, featuring flat cardboard characters whose behaviour is presented without any background, explanatory information. The guitar-playing layabout in *Lifeline* is not a person but an enigmatic caricature, and as such he cannot pose a genuine moral problem or create a genuine moral situation. Only a fully documented case study could begin to achieve the depth necessary to create a situation about which meaningful judgments could perhaps be made.

If these are some of the problems surrounding third person judgments about hypothetical moral situations which involve a conflict of principles, are we on safer ground with first person judgments? What objections, apart from the confusion between prediction and decision, are there to presenting children with a hypothetical principle versus principle dilemma and asking, 'What would you do?'

Behind this procedure there appears to lie a commonly held assumption about how we come to make moral judgments and decisions, namely by applying to actual situations principles which we have previously in some way learned and accepted. To decide, then, which principle to apply in a particular situation, hypothetical or actual, the child presumably works out which principles are relevant to that situation, ranks them in order of priority, and chooses the relevant principle with the highest rating.

This model of principle-application, though, is not necessarily a helpful one for moral development or moral education. Hirst sums up the problem neatly when he asks whether moral reasoning works from general principles to particular cases, or from particular cases to general principles. Taking issue with the proponents of situation ethics, he argues that principles must be logically prior to situations, which seems to support the principle-application model.[8]

Yet even if general moral principles do have this *logical* priority over particular cases, this does not mean that the *psychological* priorities have to be similar. In other words, as far as children's moral development is concerned, it could well be that principles can only be derived and learned from particular cases and situations, which are thus in one sense prior to the principles. Indeed, it is difficult to see how a child could actually arrive at and accept a principle, without having first experienced situations to which that principle could be applied. How could a child arrive at the principle of truth-telling without having first experienced situations which offered opportunities for telling the truth or for lying, and without having these possibilities explained to him? It seems an unjustified assumption to suppose that a child can necessarily tackle a hypothetical moral problem by deciding which of his principles, already worked out and ranked in order of priority, is most applicable.

Furthermore, it is arguable whether general principles have even a *logical* priority over particular cases, as Hirst claims. Logical interdependence may be a more helpful notion than logical priority, for moral principles and moral situations appear to be meaningful only in relation to each other. The principle of truth-telling, for example, can be given meaning only by reference to actual situations in which we are called upon either to tell the truth or to lie, and conversely such situations can be seen as moral situations only if we recognize that moral principles are applicable to them. The actual situational experience, then, and the applying of a principle are logically interdependent elements in moral reasoning and moral action.

It follows from this that principles can be learned only in the context of direct situational experience in which it is explained to the learner how the principle may be relevant. The principle of respect for others' property, for instance, can be learned by a child only as a result of experiences such as losing one's school cap, being tempted to take someone else's cap to replace it, and being shown how that situation can be interpreted in terms of principles.

As far as the *learning* of moral principles is concerned, therefore, it does not look as if the presentation of hypothetical moral situations can contribute very much, because a hypothetical situation by definition cannot provide actual situational experience, which is an essential element in the learning of moral principles.

If, however, it is claimed that hypothetical moral situations involving a conflict of principles can be used to help children *refine* principles which they have learned as a result of direct experience, this is still open to similar objections. Any refining process must involve some alteration; the principle's field of application will be broadened or narrowed as other factors are brought into consideration and their relevance judged. But these factors are situational and their moral significance can properly be evaluated only at first hand. My evaluation will depend upon how I see the situation, and that will, in turn, depend upon how I feel about it and how the various factors weigh with me.

Principle versus principle conflicts, therefore, cannot be rehearsed beforehand any more easily than principle versus inclination conflicts, and for similar reasons. My weighing of the principle of respecting others' property against the principle of alleviating suffering can only take place in a situational context in which real people are involved, and cannot be divorced from my feelings towards those people, e. g. the druggist, my wife, etc. Yet situational feelings of this kind cannot be experienced secondhand, as was argued earlier. For these reasons it is also probably overoptimistic to expect that this kind of hypothetical moral situation will give testers much indication of a child's level of moral development, as the hypothetical situation provides a different form of experience from the actual situation.

This account has tried to examine some possible weaknesses

inherent in the hypothetical moral situation approach to moral education as it is sometimes used by teachers and researchers, but this is not to say that such an approach is devoid of educational justification. It could well be argued that discussion of moral conflicts and dilemmas is valuable for young people, particularly if the issues can be related to incidents within their own experience. Such discussion may improve children's cognitive grasp of the possible dimensions of a moral dilemma by helping them to see how various people's interests and feelings are at stake, and how the problem may allow of differing interpretations. It would be reasonable to hope that this might result in better-informed and more sophisticated moral judgments being made by the children.

To grant this point, however, is not to grant that this approach will produce 'improvements in behaviour as well as in attitude' or encourage 'a willingness to act upon one's beliefs', as McPhail claims. It is easy to fall into the trap of assuming that the relationship between a hypothetical judgment and a situational judgment is a straightforward and direct one. This assumption has here been questioned by the suggestion that a hypothetical situation must lack some of the necessary features of a moral situation, and that the two cannot thus be parallel. If there is anything in this suggestion, teachers and researchers concerned with moral education will need to explore more carefully the possible limitations of the hypothetical moral situation approach and to place less unquestioning reliance upon it.

The peculiarities of hypothetical moral situations which have been examined in this chapter also have interesting implications for the judgment/action problem in moral education. Many moral judgments are hypothetical or non-immediate in the sense that they refer to a situation, usually in the future though sometimes in the past, which is different from the situation in which the judgment is made; though it is, of course, quite possible to be faced with an immediate moral decision on the spot. The hypothetical type of moral judgment concerning a future situation, however, is the one most likely to be made or discussed in a moral education programme, and if the argument of this chapter is correct, there will be all sorts of reasons why such judgments may have only a tenuous connection with the action taken in a real-life situation. We have seen in this chapter that these reasons may be varied and complex, and teachers must accordingly beware of making crude assumptions, either:

(a) that pupils will necessarily behave in a future situation as they now judge they (or somebody else) ought to behave in a hypothetical situation, or

(b) that any failures to behave in this way can be simply explained in terms of those pupils' 'weakness'.

NOTES AND REFERENCES

(1) See e.g. Hartshorne, H., and May, M. A. (1928–30) *Studies in the Nature of Character* (New York: Macmillan).

(2) Kohlberg, L. (1984) *The Psychology of Moral Development* (San Francisco: Harper & Row).

(3) Schools Council Moral Education Curriculum Project (1972) *Lifeline* (London: Longman).

(4) McPhail, P., Ungoed-Thomas, J. R., and Chapman, H. (1972) *Moral Education in the Secondary School* (London: Longman).

(5) I owe this point to a memorable lecture by Renford Bambrough on 'The teaching of philosophy' (1971).

(6) Winch, P. (1965) The universalizability of moral judgments, *Monist* **49**, 196–214.

(7) Hare, R. M. (1963) *Freedom and Reason* (Oxford: Clarendon Press).

(8) Hirst, P. H. (1969) 'The foundations of moral judgment' in Macy, C. (ed.), *Let's Teach Them Right* (London: Pemberton).

FURTHER QUESTIONS FOR CONSIDERATION

(1) What are the ethical and practical objections to placing children in real situations of moral conflict? How, if at all, might these objections be overcome?

(2) What can be done to increase the immediacy of a hypothetical moral situation?

(3) Do you agree that the actual motivational effect of states of mind like fear, love, grief and awe cannot be properly appreciated second-hand? What exactly is happening when we are 'moved' by a novel or a play?

(4) Does it follow from Winch's argument that there can be no objective moral principles or standards?

(5) Does the same follow from Hare's suggestion that all situations are in effect unique?

(6) Do you agree that children can only learn moral principles in the context of direct situational experience?

(7) Do moral decisions always involve the conscious application of moral principles?

Chapter 6

How to Combat Children's 'Weakness of Will'

At several points in earlier chapters it has been suggested that 'weakness' can often be a misleading term to use to explain why people do not always behave as they believe they ought, and it is for that reason that 'weakness of will' is placed within quotation marks in the title of this chapter. The complexity of the relationship between beliefs and behaviour warns us against expecting that any one single, simple explanation can be given for breakdowns in that relationship. Consequently, if moral education is to try to address the problem of such breakdowns, the methods it uses will have to reflect this complexity by paying attention at the very least to both sides of the relationship, i.e. to children's beliefs and their behaviour.

A crude distinction can be drawn here between what could be labelled 'verbal' and 'practical' methods of moral education. The former will refer to occasions when adults either talk to children or encourage them to talk among themselves about moral matters, and could include such activities as:

(i)   describing to children a pattern, model or ideal of behaviour, and urging them to strive to achieve it.
(ii) teaching and explaining how moral judgments are made and how moral reasoning is conducted.
(iii) discussion of moral issues.

The latter will refer to activities in which the child is either the agent or the recipient, and which are intended to influence his moral thinking, beliefs and behaviour. These could include:

(i)   rewarding and punishing, aimed at encouraging or discouraging certain types of behaviour.

(ii)   encouragement to follow the example of somebody who is considered to exemplify moral qualities.

(iii)   role-play and drama to aid 'identification' and 'empathy' with others.

(iv)   various allegedly 'character-forming' activities such as sports and games, hobbies, projects of the 'Outward Bound' type, and community service.

I have examined elsewhere the possible advantages and disadvantages of these and other methods as means of combating children's 'weakness of will',[1] and will not repeat the detailed arguments here. A reasonable conclusion, however, seems to be that just as the phenomenon of 'weakness of will' cannot be interpreted simply as a case of either 'misjudgment' or 'misbehaviour', so can it not be combated by either a predominately 'verbal' or a predominantly 'practical' approach. Constant interaction is needed between practical experience, on the one hand, and linguistic commentaries upon that experience, on the other. A number of important points follow from this.

(a) The 'weak-willed' person fails to act upon his beliefs that certain reasons and principles (of a moral or non-moral kind) are justificatory. But, although the *logical* essence of weakness of will may be thought of as a failure to translate one's principles into action, it does not necessarily follow that children's learning within this area conforms *psychologically* and *chronologically* to a 'two-stage' model of first acquiring principles and then putting them into practice by applying them to particular situations.

This point was made in the previous chapter in connection with hypothetical moral situations, where it was argued that children learn justificatory principles in the context of direct situational experience, in which explanation is given of how the particular principle is relevant. This interdependence of principles and experience adds weight to the argument in favour of constant interaction between 'verbal' and 'practical' methods. Situational experience of problems and dilemmas, and participation in activities which can be previously or subsequently discussed, examined, interpreted, explained, criticized and evaluated verbally, will at least take some account of the complex logical and psychological features of 'weak-willed' behaviour.

(b) Because the 'weak-willed' person wants to do what he does more than what he believes he ought to do, 'anti-weakness' methods must pay particular attention to the development and modification of children's wants. A sequential programme of moral education might be devised in this connection based upon Kohlberg's account of motivational levels.[2] Thus, rewards and punishments would be used with young children to encourage them to want to do what they might otherwise not want to do; at the next stage more use would be made of the child's desire for adult and peer-group approval, his tendency to follow examples, and his increasing ability to 'identify' and 'empathize' with others; and finally the attitudes and beliefs so acquired might be systematized into a framework of more abstract, justifying principles, incorporated in the child's 'conscience'. Habit-formation of some kind would be the aim at each stage, and extrinsic forms of motivation would give way to intrinsic ones as the child came to want to do what he believed he ought to do *because* he so believed rather than because of external sanctions.

Such a programme recalls and gives some content to Aristotle's dictum concerning the role of habituation in moral learning: '. . . it is a matter of real importance whether our early education confirms us in one set of habits or another',[3] and also to Bradley's account:

> The child is taught to will a content which is universal and good, and he learns to identify his will with it, so that he feels pleasure when he feels himself in accord with it, uneasiness or pain when his will is contrary thereto, and he feels that it is contrary. This is the beginning of personal morality. . . .[4]

Acting as a result of an acquired habit, or even principle, suggests a certain lack of conscious reflection and deliberation at the time of the action,[5] which could constitute an advantage rather than a disadvantage in situations where 'weak-willed' behaviour is likely to occur. The longer a child (or an adult) thinks about the pros and cons of acting as he believes he ought in a particular situation, the more he may dwell upon the attractions of the countervailing factors and the more heavily they may weigh with him. Habits, then, can serve a useful 'anti-weakness' purpose in cutting short deliberation and initiating action *before* the allure of counter-inclinations becomes too great, while principles can do a similar job by providing a summary moral justification for a course of action which can be implemented *before* other considerations pose any great threat of temptation.

The building up of habits in this kind of way will be equally important in combating 'non-moral' instances of 'weak-willed' behaviour in children. Procedures like sensible eating and drinking, looking after one's teeth, and taking regular exercise can be established at an early age, before the justificatory reasons for them are fully appreciated. Similarly, the habits of careful, conscientious working can be learned by young children initially on the basis of rewards and punishment, until the procedures come to be 'second nature' and are thus relatively impervious to countervailing factors.

(c) Moral education can, of course, go on anywhere and need not be restricted to school activities and structured teaching programmes. An interesting question now arises, however, as to whether the best context for methods of combating moral 'weakness' is likely to be found in timetabled 'moral education' lessons, or in the general life and organization of the school, or in non-school activities and experiences. Each of the three contexts seems able to contribute something of value.

'Moral education' lessons in school are probably the best way of dealing systematically and thoroughly with features of moral discourse and the methodology of moral reasoning. The fact that school time is allocated to teaching and discussion about moral questions should also emphasize their seriousness and complexity. One danger of this approach, however, is that it may imply that 'morality' is 'done' at certain times of the week, like history or geography, and if this impression is given, moral 'weakness' may even be encouraged as a result of increasing the apparent remoteness of 'what we talk about in Moral Education' from 'what happens in real life'. (A similar problem exists with regard to 'Health Education' as a school subject.) Less formally structured school activities and experiences reduce this risk, though at the cost of providing a less comprehensive, explicit treatment of moral questions. Games, clubs, societies, projects, rituals, traditions and the everyday interpersonal transactions which go to make up the life and ethos of a school provide opportunities for every kind of 'anti-weakness' method, and what is taught and learned by these means stands a good chance of becoming 'internalized' in the form of habits, for these transactions are not 'mere talk' but constitute a large part of schoolchildren's daily life. For many children, however, 'real life' starts at the school gates, and if 'anti-weakness' methods are to have any effect on children's behaviour out of school, they will obviously need some reinforcement in out-of-school situations, particularly in the home.

Probably more important, though, than whether 'anti-weakness' methods are used formally or informally, or in or out of school, is whether or not they form a consistent pattern of social learning and experience, the continuity of which encourages identification, example-following and habit-formation. This point will be developed further in (d).

(d) Many moral concepts derive their logical point from the pre-supposition that the moral life is relatively difficult to lead. Moral behaviour is for most of us a struggle, an effort and an arena of conflict. Moral duties, obligations and ideals represent standards and goals which are, because of the nature of morality and of human beings, difficult to attain.

However, it does not follow that one learns *psychologically* to lead the moral life through a process of constant struggle. Difficult skills are not acquired, nor difficult tasks achieved, by letting one's mind dwell at the outset on the magnitude of the problems and obstacles, or by setting oneself objectives which one will, in all probability, fail to attain. Success is more likely to result if one concentrates first upon the easier components of the skills to be acquired, practises these until they become 'second nature', and builds upon them to achieve further, more difficult, but still realistic goals. One does not *learn* how to climb the south-west face of Everest by initially *trying* to climb the south-west face of Everest.

Similarly, one does not learn to combat moral 'weakness' by being faced initially with a stark conflict between obligation and inclination, and by trying, in Benson's words, 'to beat the passions into submission in the interests of morality'.[6] Children learn the initial requirements of morality by learning to behave in ways

which please others whom they wish to please, and which consequently please themselves; they acquire habits because they *want*
to acquire them, not because they have struggled to subdue their
wants in favour of something which they do not want. Children
in their early years become aware of moral demands through
the personal mediation of adult prescriptions, and they learn to
conform to (at least some of) these demands because of benefits
and satisfactions which accrue to them as a result; they become
moral beings by gradually conforming to social expectations rather
than by fighting constant and lonely battles against temptation
and inclination.

(e) Finally, if the above sketch is roughly correct, an important
general implication for 'anti-weakness' methods of moral education will follow. To be effective, such methods will have to be
viewed and practised not simply as a particular set of educational
techniques designed to achieve a specific, limited goal, but rather
as an integral and constitutive element in the social traditions
within which the child is growing up. Habits are formed, examples
followed, and identifications made most easily within a social form
of life which allows continuity and consistency of experience and
also predictability of expectations. Participation in a variety of
social institutions, then, such as school, the youth club, the sports
club, the church, Cubs and Brownies, Scouts and Guides, etc.
will provide opportunities for 'verbal' teaching, explanation,
instruction and discussion to interact with 'practical' experience
of rewards and punishments, example-following and 'character-
forming' activities, for such institutions are characterized by particular procedures, values and goals which are communicated to
new members and reinforced for existing members by this interaction of the 'verbal' and the 'practical'. If the child is made to
feel a real member of such social institutions, and if within that
institutional context adults deliberately expose him to the kind of
linguistic and situational experience which has here been
described, little more can be done to 'strengthen his will'.

NOTES AND REFERENCES

(1) Straughan, R., (1982) *I Ought to, But . . . : A Philosophical Approach to the Problem of Weakness of Will in Education* (Windsor: NFER-Nelson), chapter 8.
(2) Kohlberg, L. (1984) *The Psychology of Moral Development* (San Francisco: Harper & Row), chapter 2.
(3) Aristotle (1953 edn) *Nicomachean Ethics* (Harmondsworth, Middx: Penguin), p. 56.
(4) Bradley, F. H. (1927) *Ethical Studies* (Oxford: Clarendon), p. 178.
(5) See e.g. Peters, R. S. (1963) 'Reason and habit: the paradox of moral education' in Niblett, W. R. (ed.) *Moral Education in a Changing Society* (London: Faber), pp. 46–65.
(6) Benson, J. (1968) Oughts and wants, *Proceedings of the Aristotelian Society* **XLII**, 172.

FURTHER QUESTIONS FOR CONSIDERATION

(1) Which 'verbal' and 'practical' methods are likely to be most successful in combating children's 'weakness of will'?
(2) What is distinctive about so-called 'character-forming' activities?
(3) What are the dangers of seeing 'habit-formation' as an aim of moral education?
(4) Should 'Moral Education' (or 'Personal and Social Education') appear as such on the school timetable?
(5) Is moral behaviour *necessarily* a struggle and an effort?
(6) Do you agree with the emphasis placed in this chapter upon children participating in a variety of social institutions?

Chapter 7

From Teaching that . . .
to Teaching to . . .

If moral education's aim is to promote children's moral learning, it will presumably involve moral teaching, for teaching is the label we normally apply to activities which are intended to achieve learning. 'Moral teaching', however, has a somewhat forbidding sound to it, and the term certainly does not feature prominently in current debate about moral, personal and social education, perhaps because it seems to carry with it overtones of authoritarian, 'moralistic' instruction and preaching. But teaching can take many forms, and by drawing some basic distinctions between these we should become clearer about the role which teaching can and should play in moral education.

What sort of teaching will the moral educator be concerned with? Will he or she be aiming to teach children *that certain things are true* (as the geography teacher might teach that Rome is the capital of Italy); or to teach children *how to do certain things* (as the mathematics teacher might teach a class how to solve quadratic equations); or to teach children *to do certain things* (as the science teacher might teach pupils to be careful when handling dangerous chemicals)? The answer will depend upon what the appropriate subject matter of 'moral education' is considered to be and, in fact, a case can probably be made for the inclusion of all three types of teaching, which suggests that there may well be no simple, unitary method of moral education.

Moreover, failing to recognize the different forms of teaching which may be involved in moral education blurs another distinction, which results in the teacher's difficulties being underestimated. Teaching children *to do X* is directly related to the particular behaviour (X) which results; for example, I can claim that I have successfully taught a child to tell the truth at all times, only if the child, as a result of my teaching, *does* in fact tell the truth at all times. But teaching *that* . . . and teaching *how* . . . are not so directly tied to the child's behaviour in this way.[1] If I successfully teach a child *that* it is wrong to steal, he will have learned *that* it is wrong to steal, but that is no guarantee that he *will not* steal on some future occasion. Similarly, if I teach a child *how to* handle fireworks safely, he will have learned *how to* handle fireworks safely, but again there is no guarantee that he *will* handle his fireworks safely on Bonfire Night. Not all forms of teaching and learning, then, necessarily lead to the required pattern of behaviour, for the propositions and skills that are taught and learned (in the 'that' and 'how' forms) may for various reasons not always be put into practice by the learner. So, by equating moral education with teaching children *to* behave in certain ways, and by ignoring the other less direct forms of teaching which may nevertheless also be important, we can make the teacher's job sound far more simple and more assured of success than it really is.

Much more, however, needs to be said about each of these forms of teaching which we have so far distinguished. Let us look at each in turn and consider what contribution it might make to the business of moral education.

(A) TEACHING THAT . . .

Teaching that certain things are and are not the case is an essential part of moral education, because one cannot make sound moral decisions without a firm basis of factual information. It will not be easy to work out what selection of information is of most use to young people in making moral decisions, as different situations will call for different factual knowledge. All that can be done is to ensure that they have that information which we predict will be of most relevance in those moral situations in which they are most likely to find themselves. Obvious areas where factual information will probably be needed include the following: safety in the home and school and on the roads, for a child's behaviour here can easily affect the lives of others, and of himself; individual and group psychology, for children of all ages need to increase their understanding of why people behave in certain ways in certain circumstances, in order that they may become better at anticipating the feelings and reactions of others, and of themselves; emotional, social, intellectual, physical and sexual development, for it is important that children realize the vast range of human differences which must be taken into account in deciding how to treat other people; and lastly, mental and physical health, for children's interpretations of 'human welfare' must be based on some understanding of what is normally considered to be healthy and beneficial. The list could be extended almost indefinitely, for *all* information is grist to the moral agent's mill, but the above areas at least suggest some starting-points for a planned teaching programme.

Is there also a place in moral education for teaching children that morality is made up of certain *rules* which they must obey? A number of points need to be made here.

Firstly, young children need to be taught what a rule is, because rules and principles are the medium through which moral language is expressed. Secondly, they will have to be given *examples* of simple rules to follow, before they can begin to formulate any for themselves. Thirdly, there is a number of such 'basic rules' (concerning non-injury, for instance), which only the most perverse of philosophers, or the most permissive of parents, would want to deny should be taught to young children. Fourthly, some form of unsophisticated but reasoned *justification* can and should be given for these rules wherever practicable, even if it takes young children some time to start to appreciate this. Fifthly, and finally, children should be taught as early as possible that rules are not proven facts but moral judgments, and as such can be rationally supported, discussed, challenged, and perhaps revised; so any moral content that is taught in the form of specific rules must be presented, as it were, *provisionally*, for moral education must aim ultimately at getting children not simply to *obey* certain rules, but to seek the *justification* for them and subject them to rational criticism.

These points indicate that, in practice, teaching that . . . is often closely intertwined with the second form of teaching – teaching how. . . . Teaching children along the lines just suggested, that there are certain moral rules which should be followed, will soon shade into teaching them *how* to form moral rules and make moral judgments for themselves. Let us turn next, then, to consider the *skills* which appear most important in moral reasoning, and the ways in which they might be taught.

(B) TEACHING HOW . . .

The first and most general feature of moral reasoning, which must be examined from the educational viewpoint, concerns the need for some degree of independent judgment and free choice to be exercised in the making of moral decisions. This is such a broad requirement (and also, of course, one which applies not only to the moral area, but to all aspects of rational thinking) that it is unlikely to be *directly* teachable in the way that more specific skills, like tying one's own shoelaces, are – although 'decision-making' is coming to be increasingly thought of as a composite ability which can be taught. Probably, however, the most influential factor in determining the development of this moral component is to be found, not in any particular set of teaching materials, but in the attitude and example of teachers and parents. Making up one's own mind in the light of relevant information, rather than merely doing as one is told, is a procedure which children appear to 'pick up' from adults who practise it themselves and expect others to practise it. Teachers and parents who complain that their children do not or cannot 'think for themselves' tend to be those who, in practice, allow least opportunity for children to work out their own conclusions and make their own decisions. Of course, this can be a time-consuming and irritating business for the adult, much slower than *telling* children what to think and do, but how otherwise are they to get the flavour of what it means to 'think for yourself', and so take the first steps towards becoming autonomous moral agents?

Two particular teaching approaches are worth mentioning in this connection, being designed partly to help children to think for themselves about questions involving values. Firstly, in Britain, the Humanities Curriculum Project, under the directorship of Lawrence Stenhouse, proposed a method by which 'controversial issues should be handled in the classroom with adolescents', without relying upon the teacher authoritatively to provide the 'answers'.[2] The method itself has proved as controversial as the issues which it was devised to deal with. It recommends a strictly 'neutral' role for the teacher, in that his task is to feed in as 'evidence' various kinds of written and pictorial material to discussions on topics such as war, education, poverty, relationships between the sexes, and law and order, *without* declaring his own opinions; his concern must be that 'the discussion should protect divergence of view among participants, rather than attempt to achieve consensus'.[3] Thus, the Project at least represents a determined attempt to get children to weigh evidence for themselves and reach their own conclusions.

Secondly, in the United States and Canada, the approach known as 'values clarification' has produced a mass of theoretical literature and practical materials, concerned with the analysis of what it means to value something.[4] The educational aim of the process is to lead children, by means of dialogue and discussion, to work out what their values are, and why they hold them. Much emphasis here is placed upon free choice; one's values are to be *chosen* from a range of alternatives, as a result of reflecting carefully upon the likely consequences and implications of each alternative, and many 'games' and simulation exercises have been constructed to aid the making of such choices.[5]

There are, then, some possible teaching strategies which might help children to make their own choices, decisions and judgments, but could any of the more specific features of moral reasoning also be taught as skills? Moral judgments are typically characterized by their generality, universality, logical consistency, objectivity, detachment and impartiality. These features are best illustrated by pointing out in negative terms what moral reasoning is *not*. The judgments and decisions with which it is concerned cannot be made arbitrarily, without any reference to general rules or principles, nor be seen as unrelated to other similar situations, nor be viewed as mere expressions of personal whims, tastes or feelings. Moral reasoning is in these respects an 'impersonal' matter, though paradoxically it is most frequently employed in making decisions about personal relationships, personal interests and personal welfare. Thus, the moral agent often has, in one sense, to make an 'impersonal', moral judgment (i.e. one that disregards the *personalities* involved, and his own feelings towards them), yet in another sense his decision must take account of how other people's personal well-being will be affected by whatever he does.

The 'impersonal' features of moral reasoning present some interesting teaching problems, particularly in connection with the so-called 'egocentric' and 'concrete' thinking of younger children. The ability to reason in general rather than particular terms, and to adopt a detached, impartial viewpoint, appears to develop relatively late, and it is an open question to what extent such abilities can be 'taught'. Kohlberg, for example, argues that direct teaching (though not 'cognitive stimulation', which he somewhat confusingly contrasts with teaching) cannot raise children from a lower to a higher stage of moral thinking.[6]

Yet certain forms of teaching seem, on the face of it at least, to provide a useful and necessary foundation for some of the skills of moral reasoning. One such approach is exemplified by the familiar response of the reproving teacher or parent – 'What would it be like if *everyone* behaved like that?' or 'How would you feel if someone did that to *you*?' Though the adult asking these questions will often not have worked out the philosophical rationale behind them, this is still an excellent way of drawing a young child's attention to the features of generality and universality, by prompting him to detach himself from his 'self-centred' perspective, and to try to imagine other viewpoints. Until the child starts to make these thought experiments for himself, by visualizing himself in the position of others, his moral development must be severely limited.

The Schools Council Moral Education Project also makes fruitful suggestions in this connection, despite its suspect theoretical foundations. Both the *Lifeline* materials, designed for teenagers, and the more recent *Startline* programme, intended for 8 to 13-year-olds, lay great emphasis upon the need for children to develop their interpersonal understanding, by trying to see other people's points of view and to put themselves into other people's shoes. This 'de-centring' process, whatever effect it may have upon children's 'considerateness', could well lead to the making of more objective and impartial judgments.

Both of the above approaches may also help to develop and refine the child's concept of 'fairness', by illustrating the 'impersonality' of moral reasoning. The notion of 'fairness' is itself a crucial one for teachers and parents to focus upon, for it is at one and the same time a basic element in even the young child's moral vocabulary, and also a moral principle of great philosophical significance, neatly encompassing most of the 'impersonal' features of morality which have been mentioned; a 'fair' decision is one which is held to be applicable to other similar situations, is logically coherent, and is arrived at in an impartial, non-arbitrary and non-subjective manner. There seems no more promising method, therefore, of giving children the flavour of moral reasoning, and of getting them to practise the skills which it requires, than by taking every opportunity to discuss with them what *counts* as 'fair' and 'unfair', and why? Concrete examples of everyday incidents can be used with young children (e.g. is it necessarily fair to punish two children in the same way for the same piece of misbehaviour?), leading to a consideration of more general applications of the principle at the later, more advanced stages of reasoning (e.g. is apartheid a 'fair' system of social organization?).

Much more detail, of course, needs to be filled in to these practical suggestions for teaching that . . . and teaching how . . . which have been outlined here, but it seems safe to proceed on the assumption that a sizeable chunk of morality's form and content is in fact teachable. Children can be taught a great deal of factual information, which is a prerequisite of making rational moral decisions; they can be taught at a young age certain basic rules, which all or most moral agents would accept and also, at an appropriate level, the reasoning that lies behind them; they can be taught how to start making up their own minds freely and reflectively about moral questions; and they can be taught how to reason about moral matters in a way which respects the 'impersonal' features of morality. These items cannot, needless to say, all be taught directly, straightforwardly, or with the immediate prospect of success. Most of them represent long-term objectives, which may be achieved only after a lengthy period of experience, practice and maturation, as well as teaching. Yet there remains plenty of scope for positive teaching, in familiarizing children with these aspects of morality, and thereby encouraging their development as moral agents.

The most difficult questions, however, still lie ahead. Even if we have succeeded in showing that we can teach children *about morality*, in the sense that we can convey to them some of the facts and rules associated with it (i.e. teaching that . . .), and some of the skills and procedures it demands (i.e. teaching how . . .), this is far from being the whole of the story. We may be able to teach children some of the information and skills which moral agents need, but can we ensure that they will *use* that information and *apply* those skills? Can we teach children not only *about morality*, but also *to be moral* and *to become moral agents*? It is to this knotty problem that we must now turn.

(C) TEACHING TO . . .

Mention was made at the beginning of this chapter of how teaching children *to* do X is tied directly to the behaviour (X) which is thereby learned, in a way in which teaching *that* X is the case, or teaching *how* to do X, are not. One can teach children a mass of information, without teaching them *to* use that information; and one can teach them how to do all sorts of things, without teaching them *to* do those things on appropriate occasions. These possibilities must be borne in mind when any form of moral education is attempted, if we are not to deceive ourselves about what has actually been taught and learned, for we saw above that children may be taught a great deal about morality, without being taught to be moral agents; they may fail to *use* the information and the skills they have acquired, when faced with a real-life moral decision, or they may fail to *act* upon the moral judgments they have formed. Teaching to . . . must, therefore, play at least as important a part in moral education as teaching that . . . and teaching how. . . .

If this distinction between the different forms of moral teaching is ignored, the result is often considerable confusion about the aims of moral education and its effectiveness. In America and Canada, for example, several moral education programmes have been based upon Kohlberg's research into moral development, but Kohlberg is predominantly concerned with moral *judgment* and *reasoning*, as will be demonstrated in Section Three, and has comparatively little to say about the factors which affect whether or not children *act* in accordance with their judgments; so, even if these teaching programmes succeeded in raising children's levels of moral reasoning, they would not necessarily be producing moral *agents*.

Can we, then, teach children to act as moral agents? The crucial factor here is not knowledge of facts or procedures, but motivation. When we fail to act as moral agents, though possessing all the required information and skills, it is usually because we do not *want* so to act. It is, unfortunately, a not uncommon human experience to believe that one ought to do something, without translating that belief into action, and such behaviour is commonly attributed to our 'weakness of will'. The most straightforward interpretation, however, of this 'weakness', which has been put forward in earlier chapters of this book, is that we sometimes simply do not want to do what we believe we ought to do. A girl may, for example, accept that there are good reasons why she *ought* to get home by the time she promised, and so prevent her parents worrying about her safety, but also be influenced by other kinds of reason, which motivate her to *want* to stay out with her friends, with whom she is having a good time.

Teaching children to be moral, then, must become a matter of teaching them to *want* to be moral. The knowledge and abilities which can result from teaching that . . . and teaching how . . . are not enough in themselves to ensure this motivation, though it will no doubt often be the case that children *will* want to make use of what they have learned, in forming moral decisions and acting upon them. Clearly, no teaching method can *guarantee* to produce the appropriate motivation and subsequent behaviour, for teaching (unlike conditioning and indoctrination) implies that the learner is a free agent, capable of accepting or rejecting what is taught; and, furthermore, the necessary 'gappiness' of morality means that there must always remain the possibility of a moral decision *not* being acted upon.

Nevertheless, if moral education is not to stay a wholly 'theoretical' enterprise, it cannot shut its eyes to the problems of teaching to . . . Such teaching cannot consist simply of the transmission of knowledge and skills, so what is it to focus upon? The answer must lie in one of the components of morality which has come to our notice at earlier points in this book, and which now calls for a more systematic analysis – the 'feeling' element.

When we *want* to do something, we feel attracted or positively inclined towards that action, because we see it or its likely consequences as desirable in some way or other. If our aim is for children to want to be moral, then, we must present moral behaviour to them in as desirable a light as possible, in order that they may feel motivated to act morally. The 'feeling' component of morality and of moral education is, therefore, of enormous practical importance, though it is also the one most open to misinterpretation and distortion.

The moral function of feeling and emotion, then; and their links with moral motivation, need careful examination. We feel that we want to act morally because we *see* a situation in a particular light, which in turn motivates us to do something about it; I may feel that I want to send some money to a famine relief project, for example, because I see this action as helping to relieve human suffering (which attracts me as a desirable goal) rather than as depleting my bank balance (which is a less motivating prospect). Our judgments and interpretations of situations thus help to determine how we feel about them, which means that moral education cannot start by directly seeking to influence children's feelings and emotions. The area of judgment and understanding cannot be by-passed in this way – not without resorting to drugs, hypnotism and brain surgery, at any rate.

Those concerned with moral education, therefore, need to arrive at a balanced view of the all-important role played by feelings in moral behaviour. Little will be achieved, for instance, by an approach which merely encourages children to 'express their emotions', in the hope that it will aid their moral development, for moral agents often have to *control* their feelings to enable decisions to be made in the cool rather than the heat of the moment. Likewise, although consideration for others represents one obvious goal of moral education, this is not necessarily best fostered by encouraging children to develop feelings of intense affection or loyalty for particular individuals, such as parents, teachers, or friends of either sex, as this might well militate against the 'impersonal' requirements of moral reasoning in situations where the conflicting interests of various people have to be weighed *impartially*.

So what can be done to teach children to want to be moral, bearing in mind these general points about moral feeling and moral motivation? Much will depend upon the age and maturity of the child, for Kohlberg has shown that children are motivated by different considerations at different stages of development. At the lower stages rewards and punishments loom large as moral incentives and sanctions and, given these 'brute facts of child development', it is difficult to see how moral education can begin to exercise any motivational effect without the use of these methods. Rewards and punishments serve to tilt the motivational scales, by directly adding to the attractiveness or unattractiveness of the behaviour in question, and therein lie their major strength and weakness. Their strength is that they may succeed in modifying the child's view of a situation, with the result that he comes to want to do that which he sees as reasonable, but which he might otherwise *not* want to do (e.g. if Johnny knows that he will be rewarded for looking after his little sister, but punished if he abandons her in the park, and goes off to play with his friends instead). The danger of rewards and punishments, on the other hand, is that the child may adopt the habit of acting simply because of the associated incentives and sanctions, and not because he appreciates any moral features of his action; his reasoning may remain at the (non-moral) level of 'What am I going to get out of doing that?' External incentives and sanctions, then, are best seen as a *pre-moral* technique, directed towards controlling and modifying children's motivations and their resultant behaviour, but unlikely to improve their grasp of *moral* reasons, or their willingness to act upon them.

What is being taught by rewarding and punishing children is not morality itself, but one facet of morality – consistency. Moral agents have to be consistent in following the rules of moral reasoning, and in translating their conclusions into action. Young children will not, of course, be able to display this degree of maturity and moral consistency, but they can at least start to form the habit of adhering reasonably consistently to certain 'basic rules', partly because of the incentives and sanctions attached to them. This need not be an unacceptably authoritarian process, for to borrow Peters' metaphor it is surely possible to give young children glimpses of the Palace of Reason while they are still finding their way around the courtyard of Habit.[7] A parent may, for example, reward Johnny for looking after his little sister, thereby helping to establish the habit of caring for the weak, while at the same time *explaining the reasons* for the reward.

The use of rewards and punishments supported by reasoned explanations, therefore, to teach children to adopt habits of consistent, rule-following behaviour, will be particularly appropriate at the earlier stages of moral development, when children are most impressed by such sanctions, and when the 'basic rules' of social living have to be transmitted. But can anything be done to encourage older children to use their increasing knowledge and ability to form moral judgments which they *care* about sufficiently to want to act upon them? Again, no teaching can guarantee such a result, but this does not mean that moral education need be entirely powerless in this respect.

Firstly, there is a sense in which older children can be taught to care about morality in a similar way to that in which they can be taught to care about any other subject which they learn about. A skilled and enthusiastic teacher of, say, history, or science, or mathematics, or language, can convey the flavour of his subject, by teaching its distinctive rules and procedures in such a way that some children will come to feel motivated to submit to this particular discipline, to adopt its patterns of reasoning, and to solve problems by applying its methods correctly. A major factor in achieving this kind of disciplined commitment will be the personal example set by the teacher, in terms of the satisfaction which he shows can be derived from mastering the subject's procedures and 'getting them right'. It should also be possible for both teachers and parents to convey the flavour of *morality* likewise, by exemplifying the challenge and satisfaction of coming to a rational, justifiable decision, about a difficult moral problem. Such solutions cannot, of course, be 'right' in the sense that mathematical solutions can be, but children can still be taught that there are better or worse, satisfactory or unsatisfactory methods of making moral decisions, and so come to *care* about the quality of their moral reasoning.

Secondly, there is the task of teaching children of all ages to interpret situations in moral terms, and to apply moral concepts correctly. Moral terms carry with them overtones of approval and disapproval, which we pick up as young children when we start to encounter moral language. 'That's stealing!' or 'That's cheating!' are not merely descriptive statements; they also express disapproval of the action in question. The moral vocabulary of children reflects this strong 'feeling' element, with the result that a child who has acquired the concept of stealing, or cheating, or cruelty, or unfairness, or laziness, or dishonesty, or greediness, will be disposed to have negative feelings towards behaviour which he classifies as an instance of any of these things; he will, other things being equal, not approve of cruelty and unfairness, and not want to be cruel or unfair himself. But how is he to recognize the instances? A child may feel opposed to the idea of 'stealing', yet not classify the action of entering an orchard to pick apples without the owner's permission *as* 'stealing'. What will be most helpful here will be the maximum amount of discussion about how concrete situations can be described and categorized, and how moral concepts can be applied to them – from the level of the 3-year-old, learning that eating more than you want so that others get less is an example of 'greediness', to that of the teenager who realizes that there is a problem over whether the term 'murder' should be applied to abortion, euthanasia, contraception and warfare.

Finally, and perhaps most importantly, moral education may be able to affect how children feel towards other people, which will in turn affect how they behave towards them. As morality is typically (though not exclusively) concerned with interpersonal transactions and relationships, this aspect of moral feeling, and the possibilities of it being 'taught', deserve special consideration.

A child may accept that there are good, moral reasons why he ought to give up his seat in the bus to an old lady, but if he positively dislikes old ladies in general, or this old lady in particular, he will be less likely to feel moved to want to act as he thinks he ought. The main motivational requirements in this area of morality are a concern for the interests of other people and a desire to promote their welfare. So what forms of moral education might make an effective contribution here?

A variety of *social experience* will be a necessity. The child who dislikes old ladies may have a very limited understanding of them, which could be improved by getting to know more about them. Closer and more regular contact with any group of people will not necessarily, of course, increase one's *liking* for them (our seat-hogging child *might* conclude from his wider experience of old ladies that they are even more cantankerous and ungrateful than he originally thought), but greater knowledge and understanding will often produce greater tolerance, as one becomes more aware of other people's attitudes and beliefs, their hopes and their fears.

Children cannot, then, learn to consider other people's interests and feelings, without knowing quite a lot about how other people live, and how they view the world. The scope for moral education here is vast; it could, for example, include many formal and informal school activities, such as producing a play or concert, running a club, taking part in school camps, expeditions, overseas trips and exchange visits, helping to organize fund-raising ventures, and taking part in community projects designed to help the elderly, the sick and the disabled. The programme of activities would naturally have to take account of the children's age and maturity, but the experience of working with others towards a common goal, and at the same time increasing one's understanding of individuals and groups whose interests and viewpoints had previously appeared remote and unimportant, is likely to have a considerable effect on most children's motivational attitudes towards other people.

This kind of social experience will not often feature as a formal part of the school curriculum, and indeed can be encouraged by parents, youth leaders and others, equally as well as by teachers. The school, however, might reasonably be expected to make a distinctive contribution in this crucial area of children's 'feeling for others', and whether or not it decides to offer a specific programme of 'moral, personal and social education', some of the more traditional elements of the curriculum are worth examining in this connection. Teachers of literature, for instance, can hardly avoid discussing with their pupils the personalities of fictional characters, and how these affect their ways of thinking and behaving. History can provide similar opportunities to analyse motives and intentions, and thereby increase children's understanding of human behaviour, while geography and social studies can illustrate a wide variety of different lifestyles and perspectives, so enlarging the child's concept of a 'person'.

Rather more controversial is the question of what religious education can and should do in this respect. The whole status of religious education on the school curriculum raises many problems which cannot be explored at length here, but what seems particularly relevant to our present investigation is the undeniable fact that religious beliefs are capable of exerting a powerful influence upon how one *feels* and *behaves* towards other people, not simply because of the divine sanctions which may motivate some believers, but also because of the distinctive view which a religion may convey of *what man is*. This is not to grant that it is the school's job to see that 'faith is established', as the Plowden Report surprisingly advocated[8] – an objective bristling with educational, theological and moral difficulties. Nor, of course, is it to accept that children should be taught a particular moral code, just because it is prescribed (or thought to be prescribed) by a particular religious authority. Yet to try to avoid these pitfalls by swinging to the opposite extreme, and depriving children of all access to religious interpretations of human experience, is equally unjustifiable, because these interpretations have been, and still are, instrumental in shaping man's view of the world and of his place in it, including his relations with his fellow men. The validity of this religious perspective certainly cannot be 'proved' like that of a mathematical theorem, but nor can it be similarly 'disproved' – which makes its status not unlike that of other highly respectable curriculum subjects, such as art or music or literature.[9]

These points support much of the current thinking about religious education, which sees the aim of the subject to be not 'establishing faith', but rather exploring the nature of religion, in terms of its various beliefs, practices and interpretations. Conceived in this way, religious education might help to develop children's concern for others by offering a wide range of alternative 'views of man' for older children to consider and discuss. 'Facts' about human nature cannot directly supply us with moral rules and principles, but there must still be some interconnections between what we think man *is*, what we think is *good* for man, and how we think we ought to *treat* other people. If I see other people as my 'brothers', or as soul-possessing 'children of God', my feelings and behaviour towards them are likely to be different from what they would be if I saw man purely as the ultimate evolutionary product of natural selection, or consisting of merely 'four buckets of water and a bagful of salts', as the materialist claims. It is essential to think deeply about what 'view of man' we believe to be most adequate and coherent, for as moral agents we cannot avoid basing our decisions about how to behave towards others partly upon our most fundamental beliefs and assumptions about the *nature* of human beings.[10]

The 'views of man' which religious education can bring to children's attention need not and should not all be 'religious' ones, which take for granted the existence of a personal God. The

Christian conception of man (or rather the various versions of it) can be discussed alongside the interpretations of other world religions and of non-religious belief-systems and doctrines. The Marxist, the Freudian psychoanalyst, and the Darwinian biologist, for example, each represent a distinctive viewpoint, while different 'views of man' are also implied in theories of racial supremacy, ecological conservation and 'alternative' technology. All such perspectives contain 'metaphysical' elements in the form of various assumptions about the nature, function and destiny of man, which go beyond mere facts about human beings which we can establish empirically. These assumptions and the values implicit in them can and should be examined carefully with adolescents, in order that they may arrive at their own 'view of man' in as informed and critical a way as possible. A start can also be made with younger children by discussing, for example, the similarities and differences which exist between man and the rest of the animal kingdom.

We have seen in this chapter how the broad scope of moral education and the multiplicity of its objectives call for a very wide range of teaching. Some of this can be categorized as teaching that . . . , some as teaching how . . . and some as teaching to . . . , but although it is useful to draw these logical distinctions, this chapter has also shown how these three forms of teaching will, in practice, often be interconnected. Morality is not just a matter of 'coming to the right judgment' or of 'modifying one's behaviour'. The constant interactions between our ever-developing beliefs and our ever-changing behaviour ensure that morality and moral education will always remain complex, difficult and fascinating areas of human activity.

NOTES AND REFERENCES

(1) Scheffler, I. (1960) *The Language of Education* (Springfield, IL: Charles C. Thomas), chapter V.
(2) Schools Council Nuffield Humanities Project (1970) *The Humanities Project: An Introduction* (London: Heinemann), p. 1.
(3) Ibid.
(4) See e.g. Simon, S., Howe, L., and Kirschenbaum, H. (1972) *Values Clarification* (New York: A & W Visual Library).

(5)   Ibid.
(6)   See e.g. Kohlberg, L. (1970), 'Education for justice' in Sizer, T. and Sizer, N. (eds) *Moral Education: Five Lectures* (Cambridge, MA: Harvard University Press).
(7)   Peters, R. S. (1974) *Psychology and Ethical Development* (London: Allen & Unwin), p. 272.
(8)   Plowden Committee on Primary Education (1967) *Children and their Primary Schools*, vol. 1 (London: HMSO), para. 572.
(9)   See Straughan, R. (1974) Religion, morality and the school, *London Educational Review* **3**, 3.
(10)   See White, J. P. (1973) *Towards a Compulsory Curriculum* (London: Routledge & Kegan Paul), pp. 48–9.

FURTHER QUESTIONS FOR CONSIDERATION

(1)   Are there 'moral facts' which can be taught?
(2)   Are there 'moral skills' which can be taught?
(3)   To what extent is it desirable or possible for a teacher to remain 'neutral' when engaged in moral education?
(4)   Why are young children so concerned with what is and is not 'fair'?
(5)   Can punishment teach children anything about morality?
(6)   Could religious education ever be thought to militate against moral education?
(7)   Should one particular 'view of man' be taught as better or more correct than others?

Chapter 8

Values, Behaviour and the Problem of Assessment

To conclude this section, which has focused upon various aspects of the judgment/action issue as it relates to moral education, two new elements will be introduced. Firstly, the concept of 'values' will be highlighted, as it has been somewhat ignored so far in this book, despite the importance which is attached to 'values education' particularly in North America and Canada. Secondly, the question of assessment will be investigated, partly because no discussion of any educational topic seems complete today without some mention of it, and partly (and more seriously) because there are very real and very interesting problems surrounding the possibility of assessment in this area, and these relate directly to the central concerns of this book.

Any teacher or researcher concerned with 'values education' needs to be clear about the problems of assessing success and failure in this area, if the dangers of self-delusion and wishful thinking are to be avoided. Flew's assertion[1] that one cannot claim to be sincerely engaged in the business of teaching unless one takes steps to find out by means of assessment what is being achieved must be applied to this field of education as much as to any other; 'values education' can demand no immunity or special treatment in this respect. The question then immediately arises, 'What are the criteria for deciding whether or not a child holds or has acquired a particular value?' which in turn raises the further question, 'What does it mean to hold a value?'

Many have tried to answer these questions in behavioural or motivational terms, arguing that a person's values are essentially revealed in how he or she *acts*, or *wants* to act. The well-known analysis of Raths, Harmin and Simon,[2] for example, reserves the term 'value' for those individual beliefs, attitudes, activities or feelings that satisfy the criteria, among others, of having been prized and cherished, incorporated into actual behaviour, and repeated in one's life. While on the opposite side of the Atlantic, a more recent account of 'Values in education' by Ormell[3] suggests that a person who holds certain values will be imbued with certain motivations, and that valuing needs to be seen in behaviour and not merely in a passive form of assent.

Now, clearly it would be absurd to deny that our moral values do often act as a strong motivational influence upon our behaviour; but this is not to admit that we must *necessarily* always act upon our values, nor even that we must *necessarily* always want to act upon them. To make these admissions, as the authors just quoted appear by implication to do, is virtually to adopt the Socratic view that to know the Good is to do it, and that no man ever willingly does what he knows to be wrong.

This Socratic view assumes that the phenomenon which we usually describe as 'weakness of will' or 'moral weakness' is a logical impossibility, for it maintains that we *cannot* fail to act as we believe we morally ought to act (given that we are physically able to do so), or to use the terminology of values theorists, that we *cannot* fail to incorporate our values into actual behaviour.

This doctrine has generated a considerable philosophical literature of its own, to which I cannot do justice here. All I can do is to offer the barest outline of an argument against the view that weakness of will is a logical, and consequently an empirical, impossibility, and that moral values must always be acted upon.

The argument is best summarized by a couple of lines from an interesting paper by Neil Cooper on oughts and wants. 'Between principles and practice, ideal and fulfilment, there will in any normal morality be a gap', claims Cooper, ' – this gappiness is an essential feature of the moral life, and is made manifest in the tension which may exist prior to action between principle and desire.'[4]

The gap which Cooper mentions has, in my view, both an empirical and a logical status. Empirically, we know as moral agents (or at least as would-be moral agents) that we can and do often fail to act in accordance with our moral judgments, values and principles. The notion of 'having a conscience' would be meaningless if this were not in fact the case, for one of the main functions of 'conscience' is to rebuke us for not having lived up to our own moral standards. Logically also, the idea of potential conflict between duty and inclination is surely central to our understanding of what morality is about; the whole point of moral rules and principles is to exert normative pressure upon us to do that which we might not *want* to do. Moral ideals are by definition hard to live up to, and our moral values serve to remind us of obligations which we might prefer to forget, and which we may well find difficult to fulfil.

It appears, then, to be perfectly meaningful to say of any adult or child that he or she holds a particular value, yet frequently fails to translate it into action. But an obvious objection might be raised at this point. Must not the person *on some occasions*, however infrequently, act in accordance with his or her values in order to qualify as really holding them? My reply to this objection would be that, while in practice we do no doubt tend to act in accordance with our values *sometimes* at least, I see no logical necessity here. Other things being equal, the presumption is that we are *likely* to act as we believe we morally ought to act, but unfortunately other things rarely (perhaps never) *are* equal when we have to make a moral decision to act in the face of various counter-inclinations. But how then, it might be asked, can we ever establish whether a person does or does not hold a particular value, if no 'behavioural' evidence is required? This certainly creates a difficult practical problem, especially for those concerned with 'values education', but it cannot be solved simply by making the word 'values' mean anything we want it to mean. We cannot re-draw our conceptual maps in order to circumvent methodological difficulties, by re-defining terms to suit our convenience. This point will be further elaborated later.

To maintain this position, however, it is necessary to offer some positive account of what it means to hold a value and fail to act upon it. Let us consider an example at this point. An adolescent values truthfulness. He believes that people ought to tell the truth rather than lies, because otherwise nobody's word can be trusted, personal relationships suffer, and communication becomes pointless. Yet on committing a serious breach of school rules, he refuses to own up to the offence, and falsely protests his innocence.

What is occurring, in this and all such cases of so-called 'moral weakness', is, as has been argued in earlier chapters of this book, a conflict between two different kinds of 'reason for action'. The boy accepts that there are good, *justificatory* reasons why he ought to tell the truth, deriving from the principle of truth-telling which he values on the grounds already mentioned. On the other hand, the situation he finds himself in contains other factors which provide him with strong *motivational* reasons for not telling the truth: he may want to avoid an unpleasant punishment, or the reproach of his parents or friends. So justificatory reasons for doing X need not coincide with motivational reasons for doing X, though of course they may do on some occasions. We do not, in other words, always do, or even want to do, that which we sincerely believe we ought to do.

To hold a value, then, is to acknowledge the validity of certain justificatory reasons for action, but what precisely does this acknowledgement entail if the reasons are not in fact acted upon? Clearly it is not sufficient merely to make verbal claims that one holds a certain value and that one acknowledges its justificatory force, for such verbalizations could, of course, be uttered by, among others, hypocrites, actors, parrots or ventriloquists' dummies. Nevertheless, in certain circumstances to announce one's verbal support of a value would count as strong evidence that its justificatory force was, in fact, acknowledged, even if no other action were taken (e.g. a child who protests that it is unfair for members of his gang to bully younger children, and who incurs unpopularity and hostility as a result, might well be said to value fairness, even if he did not actively intervene, with the odds stacked against him, to try to stop the bullying). If the justificatory reasons are not acted upon, however, one necessary condition of the value in fact being sincerely held is surely that its holder must feel some guilt or shame at his failure. The adolescent in the earlier example could hardly be said to value truthfulness if his failure to own up and his false protestations of innocence were not accompanied or followed by some pangs of conscience and remorse. This criterion does not fully solve our problem though, for Thalberg has drawn attention to the fact that 'the person who genuinely feels remorse . . . is a person who is disposed to act differently in the future'.[5] So remorse can be used as an alternative criterion to action in deciding whether a person holds a certain value or not, only if it is recognized that remorse itself requires some *eventual* attempt to act differently if it is to count as genuine; repeated displays of remorse with no corresponding efforts to improve one's behaviour will soon fail to carry conviction. Yet this does not mean that feelings of guilt, shame and remorse are not useful indicators *on any one particular occasion* that a sincerely held value has not been acted upon.

Such feelings, then, may provide in certain situations a valid alternative criterion, though again they need not yield any overt, behavioural evidence of their existence; guilt and remorse are complex emotions, and it is quite possible to suffer their pangs without making public confessions or resorting to hair shirts and self-flagellation. Similarly, there are not even any necessary *motivational* implications here. If I feel remorse for not having told the truth, I may *wish* that I had told the truth, but this does not entail that I *wanted* to tell the truth at the time, nor that I *shall want* to tell the truth on a similar occasion in the future. My genuine remorse indicates only that I believe I *ought* to have told the truth, i.e. that I acknowledge the reasons supporting my belief to have justificatory validity, though not necessarily any motivational force.

Failing to act upon a value, therefore, and even failing to *want* to act upon it are not adequate indicators that the value is not in fact held. Feelings of guilt and remorse can sometimes supply an acceptable alternative criterion, but there can be no simple, universally applicable, behavioural test to determine whether person X does or does not hold value Y. Such a judgment can only be made with any confidence by one who knows a great deal about person X, and certainly not on the basis of a few isolated pieces of behaviour. In some cases it will be extremely difficult, if not impossible, to make the judgment at all, but the inconvenient fact that holding value Y cannot be equated with the performance of particular observable actions must not lead us to assume that person X does not therefore hold value Y. This conclusion clearly creates enormous practical problems for teachers and researchers concerned with 'values education', but these are unavoidable if it is indeed *values*, and not something else, that they are talking about.

At least three important educational and methodological implications follow from all this:

1. Teachers and researchers cannot expect to obtain a full and accurate picture of what values children hold merely by observing their behaviour. The fact that a child is seen to act dishonestly does not necessarily mean that he does not hold the value of honesty in the sense already described. Indeed, one might reasonably assume that children, in so far as they are still *learning* about values and are relative newcomers to the domain of moral discourse and experience, will find it *more* difficult than adults to act in a consistent, principled manner, and will therefore often reveal greater discrepancies between their developing values and their actions. We do not expect children who are learning science, for instance, to be able from the start to act consistently in accordance with the scientific values of precision and objectivity which form an integral part of the activity into which they are being gradually initiated, so why should we have different assumptions about the learning of *moral* values?

2. The possible conflict between justificatory and motivational reasons, outlined above, should be explained to children and discussed with them in suitably concrete terms, with reference to their own experiences. To discuss with a child why he wanted to tell a lie when he believed he ought to tell the truth, and to increase thereby his awareness of the possibly conflicting pressures of motivational and justificatory considerations, will be more educationally valuable (and perhaps more practically effective) than simply to interpret the incident as a case of moral weakness and failure, to which reproach and censure are the only appropriate responses. This approach may not increase the likelihood of the child acting upon his values (though it could do so in some cases), but it will at least bring to his notice a crucial feature of morality, and contribute to his understanding of moral values. The alternative is to pretend to children that the moral life is much easier to lead than it really is – a course which will only lead to despondency, or perhaps to cynicism, when the inevitable moral failures occur. Saints and angels may be able always to translate their values into action, but for ordinary mortals morality is just not like that, and this important fact should not be concealed from children.

3. Finally, unless the need is recognized for more philosophical

analysis to be done on the concept of 'values' and on what it means to 'hold a value', there is a danger that 'values education' will proceed on the blind assumption that values are self-evidently to be identified behaviourally, and that holding a value is to be equated with performing particular, specifiable actions. Such operational definitions, though seductively convenient, can be highly misleading, as has become evident in the testing of so-called 'intelligence' and 'creativity'. The temptation for the educational researcher, and even the teacher, is to establish unambiguous, quantifiable, behavioural criteria which he can then rely upon to demonstrate the presence or absence of whatever it is he is trying to investigate or assess. But the assumption that such criteria *must* exist is an unjustifiable one, for the very nature of what is being investigated or assessed may be such that no clear-cut, behavioural evidence of it is necessarily to be expected. Intelligence and creativity may not be measurable in this way, with the result that what is in fact measured could be something very different from what we normally understand intelligence and creativity to be. In this way a gap can easily open up between the educationist's concepts and our ordinary language concepts, which can have serious consequences if neither the educationist nor the ordinary language user realizes what is happening.

My suggestion is that the concept of values is now starting to suffer this fate because of the methodological demands being made upon it by 'values educationists'. Because cheating tests, for example, are relatively easy for psychologists to devise and apply, a child's behaviour in such a test comes to be taken as a sure indicator of whether or not he 'values honesty'. Yet a child may cheat in a test for a wide variety of reasons, many of which may not be logically incompatible with his 'valuing honesty'. Moreover, the child who wrestles long but unsuccessfully with his conscience before yielding to the temptation to cheat and who feels ashamed at his lapse, may well be said to 'value honesty' far more than another less intelligent and less imaginative child to whom the possibility of cheating has not even occurred.

There can, therefore, be no simple and direct correlation between holding a particular value and performing a particular piece of behaviour, because values are just not like that. No doubt it is often convenient for researchers and teachers to assume otherwise, but if 'values education' is really to be concerned with values rather than with some obscure, operational construct, we must avoid legislating the meaning of values in such a way as to over-simplify and distort the very nature of the moral enterprise which we are trying to convey to children.[6]

NOTES AND REFERENCES

(1)   Flew, A. (1976) *Sociology, Equality and Education* (London: Macmillan), chapter 6.
(2)   Raths, L., Harmin, M., and Simon, S. (1978) *Values and Teaching* (Columbus, OH: Merrill).
(3)   Ormell, C. (1980) 'Values in education' in Straughan, R. and Wrigley, J. (eds) *Values and Evaluation in Education* (London: Harper & Row), chapter 6.
(4)   Cooper, N. (1971) 'Further thoughts on oughts and wants' in Mortimore, G. W. (ed.) *Weakness of Will* (London: Macmillan), p. 225.
(5)   Thalberg, I. (1963) Remorse, *Mind* **LXXII**, 545–55.
(6)   An earlier version of this chapter was read at the World Congress in Education on the theme of 'Values and the school', held at the University of Quebec at Trois-Rivières, Quebec, Canada, in July 1981. I particularly wish to acknowledge Chris Ormell's detailed, critical comments on that paper.

FURTHER QUESTIONS FOR CONSIDERATION

(1)   How are values related to moral judgments and moral beliefs?
(2)   What would be good evidence that a particular value was 'prized and cherished'?
(3)   What sort of 'motivation' do values exert?
(4)   What is the difference between guilt and remorse? How do we know that a person is feeling guilt or remorse?
(5)   At what age or stage of development can we say that children begin to 'hold values'?
(6)   What significance should we attribute to a child's behaviour in a cheating test?
(7)   What are the strengths and weakness of 'values clarification' as a method of moral education?

Section Three

Chapter 9

The Development of Moral and Religious Ideas and Behaviour

Moral education, which has been the focus of attention in Section Two, is subject to all kinds of constraints and limitations, and the most fundamental of these can be labelled 'developmental'. Teaching in any area has to take account of what is developmentally possible. However skilled and enthusiastic an infant teacher may be, she is unlikely to have much success in teaching her pupils the theory of relativity, or textual criticism or calculus. But what *is* developmentally possible? What are the 'facts' of development and what theories provide the best explanations of those 'facts'? These questions are particularly relevant to the areas of morality and religion, where much recent work has been done on developmental issues. This section will concentrate upon this work and examine its significance for the central topic of this book – the relationship between beliefs and behaviour. In this chapter we shall set the scene by looking at what is involved in 'moral and religious development'.

We all, whether aged seven or seventy, represent at this moment in our lives the results of our prior 'development'. Individual human beings are in a constant state of change; such changes are normally called 'development', in ordinary language usage at least, when we *approve* of them in some way.

Two of the most fundamental ways in which individuals change or develop are in their view of the world and of their actions within it. Show a picture of a starving refugee child to a baby and to a 15-year-old. Both will 'see' the same picture in that their optical nerves receive the same stimuli, but there the similarity of the experiences ends. The baby may well react to the colours and shapes of the picture, but the teenager will normally be able to *interpret* the pictorial data *as* a starving refugee child by applying the *concepts* of hunger, homelessness, deprivation, need, etc. to the situation as portrayed. These concepts, in turn, carry with them emotional and motivational overtones which may lead the teenager to think that something ought to be *done* about the situation – even that he should himself do something about it, perhaps. We develop, then, in the way that we both conceptualize our experiences to interpret the world and use these conceptualizations to motivate us and provide us with reasons for acting in a particular way.

THE NATURE OF MORALITY AND RELIGION

Morality and religion feature prominently in both of these aspects of development. Firstly, they each possess their own sets of distinctive concepts which we can use as templates to fit on to our 'raw' experiences and so produce particular kinds of interpretation; and secondly, these interpretations often contain implicit prescriptions in favour of certain actions and against others.

Let us take an example from both the moral and religious areas to illustrate these features:

a. A child sees his friend enter a garden and take some apples off a tree. This 'raw' experience can become a moral situation if appropriate moral concepts are applied to it. So if the garden belongs to a stranger who has not invited the boy to pick apples, the concepts of ownership, property, permission, trespassing and stealing could be used to interpret the situation. Such concepts are not merely descriptive; they also convey values and norms – e.g. trespassing is entering an area where one has no *right* to be, and stealing is the *wrongful* taking of another's property. To conceptualize the incident in such moral terms, therefore, is to acknowledge these evaluative, prescriptive overtones, which suggest that there are moral reasons for not trespassing or stealing in normal circumstances. This does not, of course, mean that the child will necessarily *act* upon those reasons by persuading his friend to return the apples.

b. A child regularly witnesses his parents thanking and seeking help from an invisible being they call 'God'. This experience needs religious concepts to be applied to it if it is to be interpreted and explained. The parents' behaviour then comes to be understood as 'prayer' or 'worship', concepts whose meaning is linked to that of other religious concepts ('God', 'grace', 'sin', 'salvation', etc.). Religious concepts, too, are not just descriptive: 'worship', for example, is what is *due* to God, and 'sin' is a *wrongful* state of affairs involving separation from God. So to conceptualize experiences in religious terms is to open oneself to the possible influence of another set of considerations and reasons in deciding what to do and not to do.

But are morality and religion distinct and separable areas of development? If so, what exactly are these areas, what are their dimensions and limits? What does it mean to 'be moral' or to 'be religious'?

These are difficult and complex questions about which volumes have been written and disagreement has been common. Two problems of particular concern to us here will serve to illustrate some of the difficulties:

1. Should morality and religion be defined in terms of particular ways of thinking, reasoning, judging and deciding, or in terms of particular beliefs, principles, values and behaviour? This distinction is usually described as being one between *form* and *content*. On the one hand, some have argued that morality is characterized by its form, which is reflected in the way in which moral judgments are made and moral conclusions reached (e.g. by appealing to general, universal principles which are then applied impartially and impersonally to justify specific actions.) On the other hand, others have felt that morality is essentially concerned with the content of particular principles and values (e.g. the pursuit of justice or the consideration of other people's interests). A similar distinction can be drawn in the case of religion between the form of religious thought and practices and the content of particular religious beliefs and observances.

2. Should morality and religion be defined in terms of judgments and beliefs or of actions and behaviour? Could a person count as being moral or morally developed, for example, on the basis of being mature in his moral judgments, logical in drawing moral conclusions or adept at considering moral dilemmas – even if he were very bad at translating his moral judgments and decisions into action? Or, alternatively, could another person be said to be moral or morally developed if he appeared to be a paragon of virtue in all he did, but never took the trouble to reflect upon the reasons and justifications for his actions? Similarly, should a person be called religious if he is conversant with religious ways of thinking and reasoning, or if he regularly participates in religious practices?

Shortage of space forbids a lengthy discussion of these two problems, which have nevertheless to be noted in any investigation of moral and religious development. All that we can do here is arbitrarily to short-cut the problems by suggesting that in each case a balance of both elements is probably required. On this view, morality and religion will have both a distinctive form and a distinctive content and will refer to both judgments and actions. This implies that development in each area will have to span a wide spectrum and that a distorted picture will result if one element is overemphasized at the expense of the other. A good example of an attempt to do justice to form, content, judgment and action within morality would be John Wilson's well-known analysis of the 'morally educated person'.[1]

But what of the *relationship* between morality and religion? If these two areas are closely connected or interdependent, then development within them will presumably reflect this connection; if they are discrete and independent of each other, then there seems little justification for considering moral and religious development under the same heading. Controversy again rages over this issue and again all that can be offered here is a provisional short-cut resolution of this complex question.

On the one hand, morality and religion certainly seem independent of each other in so far as each has its own distinctive language, concepts and procedures ('sinful' is not, for example, the equivalent of 'morally wrong')[2]; on the other hand, religion and morality are both essentially concerned with how people ought to behave. Our moral treatment of others is largely determined by what we believe is good and ultimately beneficial for them, and that in turn will depend upon our view of the nature of human beings – e.g. are they my 'brothers' and 'sisters', sharing the same Father, or just a random collection of atoms and molecules? It seems, then, that morality and religion are in certain respects independent of each other but in other respects are closely interlocked. If this is true, the relationship between moral and religious *development* is likely to follow a similar complex pattern.

DEVELOPMENT IN MORALITY AND RELIGION

So far we have been struggling to get to grips with the terms 'moral' and 'religious', without paying much attention to the notion of 'development'. But what exactly is thought to be 'developing' in these areas of our experience? From what and into what is this development taking place? The importance of conceptual development was mentioned earlier, but we have also seen that there are more dimensions to morality and religion than just the conceptual one.

The very idea that children (and adults) do 'develop' in terms of morality and religion probably runs counter to the common-sense assumptions of many people. Many parents and even teachers hold a relatively uncomplicated view of how children become moral and/or religious: children learn what is right and wrong by being told firmly and unambiguously what *is* right and wrong, and by having this instruction clearly reinforced by various forms of reward and punishment, thereby coming to conform to a moral and/or religious code and to acquire the appropriate virtues.

This common-sense view is inadequate on several counts:

1. Learning to conform to a particular code cannot be the sum total of morality or religion, for this is to overemphasize behaviour at the expense of judgment and reasoning. No behaviour can, in itself, count as moral or religious, without reference being made to the conceptions and motives underlying it.

2. The value and importance of obedience in morality and religions is over-estimated. It may often be the mark of a moral or religious person *not* to do as he is told, for the

dictates of an authority can never conclusively define what is morally or religiously 'right' and 'wrong'.[3]

3.   There is a considerable amount of evidence that children do not learn and progress in these areas primarily through the medium of direct instruction, and that 'development' is indeed the most apposite word to describe the process. This evidence will now be briefly reviewed by referring selectively to the work of a few representative key figures: this survey is, of course, merely illustrative and by no means comprehensive.

Jean Piaget was one of the first researchers to probe the notion of 'moral development' in depth, and his studies though frequently criticized and challenged have been highly influential. From a series of interviews with Swiss children he constructed a complex theory of moral development which interlinked with his more general theory of intellectual development.[4]

Piaget identified two distinct types of morality, which he labelled 'heteronomy' and 'autonomy'. At the heteronomous stage young children were found to regard rules of various kinds as absolute, sacrosanct and inviolable ('It's right because the rule says so'). Their moral judgments at this stage were similarly inflexible, determining the rightness or wrongness of an action in terms of its physical consequences and disregarding the motives and intentions of the agent ('It's worse to drop a pile of plates accidentally than to smash one deliberately'). As children learned to co-operate more with their peers and to gain greater understanding of other viewpoints, they developed towards the autonomous stage. Here rules were freely chosen and internalized when the reasoning behind them was appreciated; moral judgments were made in the light of situational circumstances and extenuating factors were allowed for ('He's too young to know better').

This developmental sequence is not, however, according to Piaget a clear-cut, all-or-nothing affair. Not everyone reaches the higher stage, and children do not always operate exclusively at the level of either one stage or the other: nor can precise ages be allotted to the stages.

More recently the American psychologist, Lawrence Kohlberg, and his associates have tried to refine Piaget's stages, and over a period of more than twenty years have built up an extensive corpus of theoretical and practical work, which has been referred to in earlier chapters.[5] As a result of cross-cultural and longitudinal studies, based on interviews using hypothetical moral dilemmas (e.g. should a penniless husband steal a drug to save his dying wife?), Kohlberg claimed to have distinguished six stages of moral reasoning, extending from childhood well into adulthood – though he later came to doubt whether the sixth stage is ever achieved in practice.

Elaborate descriptions of all aspects of these stages are offered, but perhaps the clearest way of illustrating them is in terms of the kind of reasons given at each stage for doing what is judged to be right. Examples would be:

Stage 1 – wanting to avoid punishment
Stage 2 – wanting to satisfy one's own needs
Stage 3 – wanting to gain the good opinion of others
Stage 4 – wanting to uphold the authority of social institutions
Stage 5 – wanting to uphold the contractual obligation of respecting the rights of others
Stage 6 – wanting to uphold a personal commitment to universal, self-chosen moral principles.

Like Piaget, Kohlberg argued that there is an invariant sequence in which everyone must pass through the stages, but that one does not always reason consistently at the level characteristic of the particular stage one has reached; many adults do not proceed beyond Stages 3 and 4. Other important claims of Kohlberg of particular educational significance within the context of this chapter include:

1. that development through the stages can be accelerated not by direct instruction, which is ineffective, but by exposing the subject to argument and discussion which exhibits elements of reasoning from the stage which is one higher than his present level.
2. that the higher one proceeds up through the stages, the more likely one is to *act* upon one's moral judgments.

The work of both Piaget and Kohlberg has generated considerable controversy, and certainly should not be accepted as established fact. Nevertheless, it does illustrate how some flesh might be put on the bones of the concept of 'moral development' and also underlines the centrality of the form/content and the judgment/action issues. Their work has given impetus to what is usually referred to as the 'cognitive-developmental' approach to moral development, and has strongly influenced other important research, which cannot be summarized here.

A cognitive-developmental approach can also be adopted towards religion as well as morality, though the work in this area is less extensive and well-known. Goldman, for example, drew upon Piaget's general theory of intellectual development to suggest a sequence as follows: from 'pre-religious' thinking at about 5 to 7 years, where religious understanding is at a fairy-tale level and concepts of God are crudely anthropomorphic; to 'sub-religious' thinking at about 7 to 11 where a more logical understanding is evident though at a concrete and materialistic level; to 'personal religious' thinking from 11 onwards, where a more abstract, spiritual level of understanding involving non-literal interpretations becomes possible.[6]

Just as Piaget's work influenced Goldman's, so more recently Kohlberg's studies have suggested a possible parallel account of religious development. Fowler, for instance, has described six stages of 'faith development', extending from a minimum age of 4 at Stage 1 (intuitive-projective faith) to a minimum of 40 at Stage 6 (universalizing faith).[7] A less abstract account is offered by Oser, which closely follows Kohlberg's stages and is worked out in terms of children's conceptions of God; thus, at Stage 1 He is seen as a physically powerful figure, at Stage 2 as one who grants benefits on a quid pro quo basis, at Stage 3 as a personal friend or caring shepherd, at Stage 4 as a law-giver, and at Stage 5 as an 'energizer' who supports autonomous moral action.[8] Such a sequence raises interesting questions about the relationship between moral and religious stages of development.

The cognitive-developmental approach which has been exemplified here is by no means the only possible one, but it has been picked out for special attention because it demonstrates a clear sense in which 'development' can be claimed to take place in morality and religion. Learning theory approaches, by contrast, are more applicable to morality than religion, and focus largely upon the shaping and modification of behaviour by rewards and punishments or by imitation of other people.[9] Appropriate behaviour is thus 'reinforced' and inappropriate behaviour 'extinguished', but such terminology does nothing to solve the problem of content. Who is to decide what is morally appropriate and inappropriate? Is it justifiable to seek to inculcate specific patterns of behaviour in children in ways which some would claim come close to conditioning? Although such approaches may perhaps be justified in terms of social control, it seems doubtful whether they have much to do with *moral development* as such, if they attempt to identify morality with limited items of behaviour and fail to look beyond that behaviour to the conceptions, beliefs, feelings and intentions which form an essential part of 'being moral' – and indeed of 'being religious'.

It is difficult, if not impossible, therefore, to speak of moral or religious development purely in terms of behaviour, and while there is an obvious danger that the cognitive-developmental approach may err in the opposite direction by overemphasizing judgmental factors at the expense of behavioural ones, that approach seems at present to offer the most illuminating picture of how individuals develop in the areas of morality and religion.

NOTES AND REFERENCES

(1) See e.g. Wilson, J. (1973) *The Assessment of Morality* (Slough: NFER). See also (1971) *Education in Religion and the Emotions* (London: Heinemann).

(2) See e.g. Hirst, P. H. (1974) *Moral Education in a Secular Society* (London: University of London Press).

(3) Straughan, R. (1988) *Can we Teach Children to be Good?* (Milton Keynes: Open University Press), pp. 6–8.

(4) Piaget, J. (1932) *The Moral Judgment of the Child* (London: Routledge & Kegan Paul).

(5) Kohlberg, L. (1981 and 1984) *Essays on Moral Development*, vols 1 and 2 (San Francisco: Harper & Row).

(6) Goldman, R. (1964) *Religious Thinking from Childhood to Adolescence* (London: Routledge & Kegan Paul).

(7) Fowler, J. (1976) 'Stages in faith: the structural developmental approach' in Hennessey, T. (ed.) *Values and Moral Development* (New York: Paulist Press).

(8) Oser, F. (1980) 'Stages of religious judgment' in Fowler, J, and Vergote, A. (eds) *Toward Moral and Religious Maturity* (Morristown, NJ: Silver-Burdett).

(9) See e.g. Eysenck, H. J. (1964) *Crime and Personality* (London: Routledge & Kegan Paul); Bandura, A. and Walters, R. H. (1963)

Social Learning and Personality Development (New York: Holt, Rinehart & Winston); and Skinner, B. F. (1962) *Walden II* (New York: Macmillan).

FURTHER QUESTIONS FOR CONSIDERATION

(1)   Does 'development' always imply improvement?

(2)   Does 'development' always imply some end-state or goal?

(3)   Could teaching children moral or religious concepts be considered as indoctrination?

(4)   Which religious concepts are not tied to a *particular* religion?

(5)   Do any religious concepts presuppose moral ones, or vice versa?

(6)   Does it make sense to think of moral development in terms of behaviour modification?

(7)   What would it mean to speak of children's behaviour as 'developing'?

Chapter 10

From Moral Judgment to Moral Action: Philosophical and Psychological Perspectives

Socrates' claim that to know the Good was to do it was denied by Aristotle on the grounds that it clearly contradicted the facts. The nature of the relationship between moral judgment and moral action has since then been vigorously debated by generations of philosophers, who have by and large tended to align themselves behind one or other of the two original protagonists. More recently, psychologists have also contributed to the discussion, presenting empirical investigations and theoretical explanations of the extent to which people's moral judgments are consistent with their actions.

Little or no attempt has yet been made, however, to set the philosophical and psychological approaches alongside each other, and to view the logical and empirical accounts from a common perspective. The aims of this chapter will therefore be:

1. to review and illustrate some disagreements which exist among both philosophers and psychologists within this area,
2. to examine possible interconnections between the logical and empirical work that has been done,
3. to explore a particular logical account of the judgment/action relationship and its empirical implications.

PHILOSOPHICAL ACCOUNTS: INTERNALISM VERSUS EXTERNALISM

Philosophical discussions of the logical relationship between moral judgment and moral action have ranged between two extreme and opposed positions, which may be labelled 'internalism' and 'externalism'. In a detailed examination of these positions, Frankena draws the distinction as follows:

> Roughly, the opposition in question is between those who regard motivation as external and those who regard it as internal to obligation . . . Many moral philosophers (the externalists) have said or implied that it is in some sense logically possible for an agent to have or see that he has an obligation even if he has no motivation, actual or dispositional, for doing the action in question; many others (the internalists) have said or implied that this is paradoxical and not logically possible . . . Internalists hold that motivation must be provided for because it is involved in the analysis of moral judgments and so is essential for an action's being or being shown to be obligatory. Externalists insist that motivation is not part of the analysis of moral judgments or of the justification of moral claims; for them motivation is an important problem, but only because it is necessary to persuade people to act in accordance with their obligations.[1]

The significance of this distinction for our present purposes lies in the fact that internalism emphasizes the logical *tightness* of the relationship between moral judgment and moral action and minimizes the possibility of a gap or inconsistency between the two, whereas externalism does the reverse. Many versions of the two positions have been expounded, as Frankena illustrates in his article, and the opposition cannot be neatly expressed in terms of the various '. . . isms' of ethical theory. These complexities will not be entered into here; a brief review of some representative arguments from the rival camps will suffice to show how widely differing views of the logical relationship between moral judgment and moral action can be held.

Extreme forms of internalism have gone so far as to assert the logical *impossibility* of a gap or inconsistency between judgment and action, so denying in effect that cases of 'weakness of will' can ever occur. Different versions of internalism base this denial on different grounds. Socrates, for example, in the *Protagoras*, employs a hedonistic argument which equates what is good with what is pleasant, and what is evil with what is painful; thus it becomes nonsense to say that a person fails to do what he knows is good because he is 'overcome by pleasure', for the best course of action is that which ultimately leads to the *greatest* pleasure and satisfaction. No one therefore willingly does what he knows to be evil (and painful), and all wrong-doing is explicable in terms not of moral weakness but of ignorance or miscalculation of the consequent pleasures and pains. Plato, in the later Dialogues, builds upon this argument, giving it a metaphysical dimension by linking it with his Theory of Ideas. Moral knowledge now becomes knowledge of the 'Idea of the Good', and a person whose education has enabled him to ascend to the mystical heights at which this Idea is apprehended will 'know the Good' in a way which makes it impossible for him not to act in accordance with that 'knowledge'.

These examples of internalist arguments also serve to illustrate the difficulty of distinguishing between logical and psychological claims at times, for it is not altogether clear whether Socrates and Plato are making strictly logical points here about *necessary* features of moral understanding or psychological points about how moral agents tend to behave. The Socratic argument in the *Protagoras*, for example, concludes, 'To make for what one believes to be evil, instead of making for the good, is not, it seems, *in human nature*'[2] (my italics), which looks, on the face of it, to be a highly dubious, empirical claim; while Plato, similarly, seems to be referring to the emotive, *psychological* effect produced by the quasi-religious experience of apprehending the 'Idea of the Good'. On the other hand, however, both accounts lean heavily upon a particular stipulative definition of 'knowledge', which distinguishes it sharply from mere 'belief' or 'opinion', and which logically requires that 'moral knowledge' leads to the appropriate action; in other words, the response of Socrates or Plato to an apparent case of a person failing to do what he knew was right would be simply to maintain, as a logical truth, 'Ah, but then he cannot *really* have known in the first place!' As we shall see later, this question of what is to count as 'moral knowledge' has become a crucial methodological one for psychologists also.

Emotivism provides further examples of internalist claims about the nature of moral judgments, where there is again difficulty in disentangling the logical from the psychological. Stevenson, for instance, has argued that ethical terms have a 'magnetism', which makes the characteristic purpose of moral discourse not to inform but to influence:

> A person who recognizes X to be good must *ipso facto* acquire a stronger tendency to act in its favour than he otherwise would have had.[3]

Such emotivist theories seem partly to be describing the psychological effect of making moral judgments, but also to be making this alleged effect a logical component of moral discourse; part of what it *means* then for a person to make a moral judgment is that he acquires a stronger tendency to act upon that judgment.

A clearer example of a strictly logical, internalist thesis is that of Hare, who makes prescription the central function of moral discourse and proposes the following chain of logical entailments. If I make a value-judgment that I ought to do X, I am thereby addressing a first-person command to myself ('Let me do X!'), to which I must sincerely assent and upon which I must act or try to act. So I cannot fail to do or try to do what I think I ought to do, provided that I am using 'ought' in its central, evaluative, prescriptive sense.[4] Hare's response to an apparent case of moral weakness would thus, like Socrates' and Plato's, be to point to an allegedly logical truth, 'Ah, but then he can't *really* have made a value-judgment in the first place!' The man who fails to act upon his value-judgment is being hypocritical, insincere, or self-deceiving in his misuse of 'ought' – or else is physically or psychologically unable to translate his value-judgment into action.[5]

Extreme versions of internalism, then, refuse to allow any wedge to be driven between moral knowledge (or judgment) and moral action. By contrast, externalism sees the relationship to be not logically necessary, but purely contingent: to recognize that X is good or obligatory *may* or *may not* be associated with wanting, trying, or committing oneself to do X. This has been characterized as a 'So what?' view of morality, i.e. the agent's judgment of what is right or good need not logically carry with it any implications for how he will act.

Externalism, as such, as been less openly espoused by philosophers than internalism, and is consequently less easy to identify with particular proponents. Echoes of the theory, however, can be heard in intuitionist accounts (such as G. E. Moore's), which hold that moral terms like 'good' refer to properties of a particular logical type. To call some thing or action or state of affairs 'good', then, is to state a 'moral fact' and to convey 'moral information', and intuitionism provides no argument for why one should ever *do* anything about these facts, or *act* upon this information. Certainly no logical relationship between moral judgment and action is even hinted at, the implication being that the relationship is merely a contingent one.

A similar implication follows from views of morality which equate what is good with certain empirical or supernatural states of affairs. If I believe that what is good is definable in terms of, for example, (i) those customs and conventions which most members of my society approve of, or (ii) that which ensures the survival of my society or of myself, or (iii) that which produces the greatest happiness for my society or for myself, or (iv) that which the law prescribes, or (v) that which God or the Pope or the Sacred Texts or the Party lays down, then these definitions will again provide 'moral facts' which I accept as accurate and informative but not necessarily of direct, practical relevance to my conduct.

Externalist arguments are also to be found in critical commentaries upon some of the versions of internalism already described. The allegedly tight, logical bonds which some internalists claim to exist between moral judgment and action have predictably been challenged, usually on the Aristotelian grounds that such claims are counter-factual. Gardiner, for instance, objects that extreme forms of internalism deny the possibility of what are apparently common human experiences:

> We have a use for expressions like 'doing what I believed to be wrong' or 'acting contrary to my principles' when there is no obvious implication of insincerity or of change of mind . . . [6]

Other writers have also used the notion of 'sincerity' to attempt to loosen the judgment/action bond, arguing that acting in conformity with a moral judgment is not the only possible criterion of the sincerity of that judgment. Remorse, guilt, shame and repentance have been proposed as alternative criteria, and Horsburgh goes so far as to claim:

> There are times when we attach more weight to remorse than we

> do to conformity in our judgments of relative fullness of assent . . .
> (and) attribute a higher degree of assent to a person after he has
> violated a moral rule than we did before.[7]

Finally, and more generally, some have maintained that the notion
of rational morality presupposes the existence of free moral agents
who must, by definition, be able to act contrary to their principles
if they so decide. Cooper's argument, for example, which was
mentioned in Chapter 8, maintains:

> Between principles and practice, ideal and fulfilment, there will in
> any normal morality be a gap – this gappiness is an essential feature
> of the moral life and is made manifest in the tension which may
> exist prior to action between principle and desire . . . It is a necess-
> ary feature of any rational morality that it should leave some room
> for moral weakness.[8]

There is, then, among philosophers no agreement over the
nature of the logical relationship (if any) between moral judgment
and moral action. This prompts us to turn to the psychologists for
some illumination of the corresponding empirical relationship, in
the hope that this may throw further light upon the vexed logical
questions. Empirical investigation is, of course, unnecessary when
logical points are beyond dispute (e.g. statistical surveys are not
required to establish what proportion of widows have lost their
husbands), but where the conceptual boundaries are more hazy,
empirical findings can sometimes suggest pointers to hitherto
unexplored logical connections; some of Piaget's work, for example, on the stages of intellectual development has been criticized
as merely enunciating logical truths for which empirical support
is superfluous, yet it is significant that these allegedly logical features of development were not paid much philosophical attention
before Piaget's empirical claims had revealed a potential seam for
philosophers to work.

PSYCHOLOGICAL ACCOUNTS: FINDINGS AND
INTERPRETATIONS

Evidence concerning the empirical relationship between the
making of moral judgments and the performing of moral actions
might be expected to help in clarifying the dispute between internalism and externalism, as suggested above. Furthermore, such

evidence merits the close attention of researchers into moral development, for questions about the 'sincerity' of a subject's verbal response (e.g. to a hypothetical dilemma), and the relationship between that response and the subject's behaviour in an actual situation, are frequently evaded or ignored, as we saw in Chapter 5.

Unfortunately, however, empirical evidence in this area is still fairly scanty, due partly to the obvious methodological problems of gathering data, and partly to one particular psychological tradition which has attempted to study moral judgment in isolation from moral action – a tradition established and illustrated in the opening sentences of Piaget's influential work on *The Moral Judgment of the Child*, quoted earlier in Chapter 4:

> Readers will find in this book no direct analysis of child morality as it is practised in home and school life, or in children's societies. It is the moral judgment that we propose to investigate, not moral behaviour or sentiments.[9]

(This is not to say that Piaget *in fact* totally ignores 'moral behaviour'. Piaget's conception of the relationship between 'theoretical' and 'practical' morality is complex, subtle and somewhat obscure. Nevertheless, Piaget has undeniably been closely identified by many with the 'judgmental' approach to moral development and moral education; though whether this identification is justified or not is a question beyond the scope of this chapter.) Moreover, what evidence there is appears *prima facie* to point in no particular direction, and interpretations of its significance are as disputed as we have seen the logical accounts to be. This will be demonstrated in the following brief review, which will take as its focus the work of Lawrence Kohlberg.

The pioneering studies of Hartshorne and May[10] exemplify clearly this lack of consensus, for they have been subjected to a wide variety of scorings and interpretations during their fifty-year history; a cautious and generalized conclusion, however, would be that they seem to show a low but positive correlation between children's 'moral knowledge' of conventional norms and their conduct in various situations which offer opportunities for stealing, cheating, and lying.

In contrast to these findings, however, Kohlberg summarizes the results of similar but more recent studies by declaring:

> Half a dozen studies show no positive correlation between high school or college students' verbal expression of the value of honesty or the badness of cheating, and the actual honesty in experimental situations.[11]

In another paper he states baldly:

> People's verbal moral values about honesty have nothing to do with how they act. People who cheat express as much or more moral disapproval of cheating as those who don't cheat.[12]

This apparent disparity between the findings of Hartshorne and May and of Kohlberg also throws into relief the all-important methodological question of what empirical researchers in this area should count as 'moral knowledge'. Kohlberg's contribution here has been to attempt to link this question with his own developmental theory of moral reasoning, claiming that when the subject's *stage* of moral thinking, rather than his mere verbal espousal of conventional moral values, is taken as the measure of 'moral knowledge', his research supports the Platonic view that 'virtue in action is knowledge of the good' and that 'true knowledge, knowledge of principles of justice, does predict virtuous action'.[13] Using data obtained from a cheating test, from Milgram's studies of obedience and authority,[14] and from a students' sit-in, he shows that far higher percentages of Stage 5 and, particularly, Stage 6 subjects translate their moral judgments into action, compared with those at the lower stages.[15] (For the sake of consistency, throughout this chapter the numbered stages will refer to the 'old' Kohlbergian sequence, as described in the corresponding references, and not to the latest proposed scoring system developed by Kohlberg with Colby, Gibbs, Speicher-Dubin, and Power.[16])

Some support for Kohlberg's thesis is provided by studies of bystander intervention. Huston and Korte, for instance,[17] cite McNamee's findings to the effect that the frequency of help given to an apparently distressed individual increased with each higher Kohlbergian level of moral development: subjects at Stage 2 helped 11 per cent of the time, at Stage 3, 27 per cent, at Stage 4, 38 per cent, at Stage 5, 68 per cent, and at Stage 6, 100 per cent.

On the other hand, Burton[18] in a review of empirical studies of honesty and dishonesty refers to the work of Podd,[19] who found no relationship between Kohlberg's moral judgment test and the level of shock administered to a 'victim' in Milgram's obedience test; and that of Krebs,[20] who found a slight positive relation between Kohlberg's scale of moral judgment and honest conduct if the moral judgment measure had been obtained *before* the conduct test, but a negative relation when the interview followed the test. Similarly, Mischel and Mischel argue, against Kohlberg, that the predictive validity for moral reasoning to moral behaviour is no more than 'modest'; referring to a study by Schwartz, Feldman, Brown, and Heingartner,[21] which was, in fact, cited by Kohlberg[22] in *support* of the reasoning/action link, they conclude:

> Correlations of the type obtained so far suggest that, overall, knowledge of individuals' moral reasoning would permit one to predict no more than about 10% of the variance in their moral behaviour.[23]

Some of these apparent disgreements can perhaps be partially resolved by noting a possible source of confusion between the notions of 'virtuous action' and 'consistent action'. Strictly speaking, it is studies only of the latter which can throw light upon the empirical relationship between moral judgment and action. For this purpose we need to know *not* whether subjects at Stage X act in ways which *we* (or 'society') deem to be morally desirable (e.g. by helping strangers in apparent distress), but whether subjects at Stage X actually translate into action what *they* judge is the right thing to do. Thus, the McNamee study cited above, for example, shows that assistance to apparent drug victims is progressively more likely to be offered as one proceeds up the Kohlbergian ladder (i.e. 'virtuous action'), not that higher stage subjects are necessarily more likely to act in accordance with their judgments than lower stage subjects (i.e. 'consistent action'); the subjects at Stage 2, who offered help least often, may have believed for various reasons that the right thing to do was *not* to help, and so may conceivably have shown *more* consistency between judgment and action than those at Stages 5 or 6 (some of whom might also for different reasons have judged that they ought not to offer help).

These complexities cannot be pursued at greater length in this brief review, the main purpose of which has been to show how Kohlberg's attempts to refine Hartshorne's and May's account of 'moral knowledge' and its relationship to moral behaviour have opened up further areas of dispute. It seems fair to conclude that, at present, there is not much more agreement over the empirical nature of that relationship than there is over its logical nature – a conclusion supported by Blasi in an extensive review of the psychological literature. Arguing that the relationship between 'moral cognition' and moral action is an extremely intricate one and that generalizations are difficult to arrive at because empirical studies have concentrated upon different aspects and interpretations of that relationship, Blasi infers there to be 'considerable support for the hypothesis that moral reasoning and moral action are statistically related'; yet he goes on to warn that this statement needs careful qualification:

> Empirical support, in fact, varies from area to area: It is strongest for the hypothesis that moral reasoning differs between delinquents and nondelinquents, and that at higher stages of moral reasoning there is greater resistance to the pressure of conforming one's judgment to other views. The support is clear but less strong for the hypothesis that higher moral stage individuals tend to be more honest and more altruistic. Finally, there is little support for the expectation that individuals of the postconventional level resist more than others the social pressure to conform in their moral action.[24]

The remainder of this chapter will try to erect a few speculative signposts in the hope that they may indicate a possible escape route from this interdisciplinary morass. Let us take as provisional premises two points of reasonable, though by no means unanimous, agreement – that the empirical relationship generally seems to be only a 'modest' one, but that a subject's *stage* of moral reasoning is a better predictor of his subsequent action than is his mere verbal espousal of, or acquiescence with, moral values and standards.

These two points, if accepted, raise four further key questions of both psychological and logical dimensions, upon which the final sections of this chapter will concentrate. The questions are:

1. Why should there be any positive relationship at all between moral judgment and action?
2. Why should this relationship be a 'modest' one?
3. Why should the relationship be stronger when the subject's

stage of moral reasoning is taken as the measure of his 'moral knowledge'?

4. Why do Kohlberg's own findings apparently fail to give complete support to his claim that 'true knowledge predicts virtuous action'? – i.e. why do even Stage 6 subjects still, at times, seem to act contrary to their moral judgments?

A POSSIBLE RESOLUTION OF THE LOGICAL DISPUTE

To investigate further the four questions just posed, we must return to the logical issue and see whether some reconciliation can be achieved between the extremes of externalism and internalism, both of which appear to embody serious weaknesses.

On the one hand, to hold that moral judgments are wholly 'external', and thereby only contingently related to moral action, is to ignore a central feature of moral concepts. Recognizing a moral obligation is not logically parallel with recognizing a face or a tune, for it is to *acknowledge* the weight and validity of non-prudential reasons and principles, which are seen as *justifying* a particular course of action. If, for example, I believe that I have an obligation not to light a bonfire in my garden when the wind will blow the smoke in the direction of my neighbour's washing on the line, I am acknowledging that the possible dirtying of my neighbour's washing is a *factor* relevant to the question whether I ought to light the bonfire or not – a factor which constitutes a valid reason why I ought *not* to light it, because I am accepting the justificatory principle that one ought not to cause avoidable annoyance to others. So I cannot truly be said to recognize the obligation which I believe to be upon me (or to make a moral judgment), unless I at the same time acknowledge the normative pressure and authority being brought to bear upon me by the reasons and principles whose justificatory force I show that I appreciate by *recognizing the obligation*. Recognizing a face or tune carries with it no prescriptive cargo of the sort entailed in recognizing an obligation, yet externalism in effect draws no distinction between these two logically separate forms of 'recognition'.

Extreme versions of internalism, on the other hand, seem to make the logical connection between moral judgment and action far too tight, so denying the possibility of yielding to temptation. I can in all sincerity believe that I ought not to light my bonfire, yet be so eager to get rid of my ever-mounting pile of rubbish on the first fine day for weeks that I go ahead and act against my principles (perhaps further encouraged by the aversion I have towards my neighbour's barking dog). After the event the sincerity of my original judgment may be confirmed by a variety of indications (e.g. I may feel guilty, embarrassed, apologetic, over-defensive, etc.). Action in conformity with a moral judgment, then, is not the only possible criterion of the sincerity of that judgment. Indeed, the conceptual geography of the word 'ought' suggests uncertainty as to whether or not the appropriate action will in fact ensue because of the likely presence of countervailing factors ('I know I really *ought* to do X, but . . .'). As Thalberg succinctly puts it, 'Ought implies might not'.[25]

Extreme versions of internalism and externalism, therefore, are equally unsatisfactory. Most of the problems can be resolved, however, by positing an internal connection *of sorts* between moral judgment and action, but not of strict logical entailment. To make a moral judgment, I have suggested, is to acknowledge that certain factors in a situation constitute reasons which justify on non-prudential grounds a certain course of action, by reference to a more general moral principle. But considerations which one sees as *justifying* the doing of X may not in practice *motivate* one to do X. Often justificatory considerations do coincide with and even help to provide motivational ones (e.g. I may want to do what I conceive to be my duty *because* I conceive it as such), but this is by no means always the case.

On this view of moral reasoning, then, it is quite possible for me, on the one hand, to form a sincere moral judgment, which acknowledges that there are good, non-prudential reasons which justify my refraining from lighting my bonfire, yet on the other hand not to *want* to refrain from lighting it because there are countervailing factors in the situation which lead me to want to get rid of my rubbish more than I want to avoid inconveniencing my neighbour. This distinction between justifying and motivating considerations, which has also been examined in earlier chapters of this book, suggests a loose, internal connection between moral judgment and action which might be partially expressed in the principle, 'Believing that one ought to do X is to do X in the absence of countervailing factors' – a principle which Griffiths describes as 'necessary to the explicability of the rational behaviour of men'.[26] According to this more moderate version of internalism, then, one does what one believes one ought to do unless one wants to do something else more, and the sincerity of one's beliefs is thus not necessarily wholly dependent upon one's acting in accordance with them.

EMPIRICAL IMPLICATIONS OF THIS LOGICAL ACCOUNT

How does this loose, internal connection which has been proposed relate to empirical findings and interpretations? To see whether any points of possible contact and compatibility can be discerned, this final section will return to the four key questions raised in the review of empirical studies, and will consider them in the light of my suggested logical account of what can be labelled 'moderate internalism'.

1. Why should there be a positive relationship at all between moral judgment and action?

A logical connection of the sort outlined above clearly gives us a warrant to expect *some* empirical, positive relationship to exist. Moderate internalism does not support the 'So what?' model of morality, implied in extreme versions of externalism, which would lead one to expect no consistent empirical relationship of any sort; rather it suggests a presumption in favour of a positive relationship, for it claims that, *other things being equal*, moral judgments will be translated into moral action (or, at least, attempted moral action).

2. Why should the relationship be a 'modest' one?

Moderate internalism is again not in conflict with this relatively undisputed empirical conclusion. The type of test situation which empirical researchers normally use is characterized (even more than situations encountered in real life) by the presence of power-ful countervailing factors, with the result that other things are decidedly *not equal* when the question of whether to act upon a moral judgment arises. Often the subject is given every oppor-tunity to cheat, lie, steal, etc., and little motivational incentive is provided to support the translation into action of any judgment *not* to cheat, lie, steal, etc. As Blasi comments, 'The experimental situations for assessing honesty have some common character-istics: In all of them some incentives to cheat are offered, and the impression is conveyed that it is safe to cheat'.[27] It is consequently not surprising if the motivational scales are often tipped against the implementation of the moral judgment, because the subject finds that situational factors are such that he wants to cheat, lie, steal, etc. more than he wants to do that which he sincerely believes he ought to do. If moderate internalism is right, there-fore, a modest but positive link between moral judgment and action is just the kind of empirical relationship which test situ-ations might be expected to produce.

3. Why should the relationship be stronger when the subject's *stage* of moral reasoning is taken as the measure of his 'moral knowledge'?

Moderate internalism also sheds some light upon this question, although at first sight it appears rather puzzling why 'principled' moral judgments (i.e. Kohlberg's Stages 5 and 6) should be more likely than 'conventional' or 'pre-conventional' ones (i.e. Stages 1–4) to be acted upon. Are not the reasons which make a judg-ment 'principled' essentially justificatory rather than motivational, and if that is so why should one be more likely to act upon a principle than upon what Kohlberg calls a 'concrete rule of action'? Should we not expect the very 'concreteness' of rules to exert a *more* direct motivational influence than less specific justificatory principles, when the chips are down and situational pressures are at work? Principles seem to possess what Cooper has called a 'cool-hour quality': '. . . a man's moral principles are those of his principles of action which in a cool hour he is least prepared to abandon belief in, however much he may be tempted to deviate from them in the heat of the moment'.[28] Yet it is in the heat of the moment that the decision has to be made whether or not to act upon our principles, and if they are indeed characterized by this cool-hour quality, this does not suggest a particularly close link between holding a principle and acting upon it.

However, if 'principled' moral judgments are, in fact, more likely to be acted upon than 'conventional' or 'pre-conventional' ones, as Kohlberg claims to have shown, there may perhaps be some other logical feature of 'principled' judgments which provides an explanatory basis for this phenomenon. The queries raised in the previous paragraph make it doubtful whether this feature could reside in the principle-versus-rule distinction itself, but that distinction, when considered alongside the further distinction between justificatory and motivational considerations, does offer possible logical support for Kohlberg's claim in the following way.

If I fail to do that which I sincerely believe I ought to do (while being fully able to do it), I am presumably not sufficiently motivated to do that which I consider to be justified. So what are the usual means by which motivation for moral behaviour is strengthened, and which are apparently lacking in such cases? These can be roughly classified as either 'self-directed' or 'other-directed' in type, corresponding to Piaget's autonomous and heteronomous levels. Praise, blame, encouragement, criticism, reward and punishment, for example, are all important forms of incentive or sanction which can be brought to bear upon the moral agent, *either* by external judges and teachers *or* by the internal verdicts of his own conscience. ('Conscience' is a notoriously ambiguous notion; it is used here and in what will follow to refer not to the causal process of experiencing guilt reactions, stemming from unexamined and unconscious sources, but to rational acts of judgment made by a moral agent about his own past, present and future conduct, based upon what he regards as justificatory reasons and obligatory principles.)

Gilligan, identifying other-directed morality as a 'shame ethic' and self-directed morality as a 'guilt ethic', argues that Kohlberg's data show that the motive for morality is to avoid either shame or guilt, and that the developmental trend described by Kohlberg is from an earlier, 'shame-motivated' morality to a later, 'guilt-motivated' one.[29] If this interpretation is correct, perhaps 'guilt', to which (according to Gilligan) one becomes increasingly sensitive as one goes up the developmental ladder, possesses certain logical features distinguishing it from 'shame', which constitutes the predominant form of motivation at the lower stages; and perhaps these features may explain why 'principled' judgments may be the most likely ones to be acted upon. Kohlberg himself comments on this motivational distinction between what Gilligan would call 'shame' and 'guilt', noting that 'intense fear of punishment does not predict resistance to temptation, whereas self-critical guilt does'.[30] However, he offers no explanation for this important finding beyond the generalized (and somewhat uninformative) statement that the difference between the two forms of motivation is a 'cognitive-structural' one, although 'in some sense, the feeling in the pit of one's stomach is the same whether it is dread of external events or dread of one's own self-judgment'.

But is there not a further, straightforward, logical distinction to be drawn here (of such simplicity perhaps that it has been lost in the complexities of psychological theory), which may explain why 'principled' subjects act upon their judgments more often than other subjects? Other-directed sanctions are avoidable; self-directed ones are not. However attractive or unattractive the prospect of an externally derived reward or punishment may be to the agent, he knows that it will materialize only if his behaviour is witnessed by others or brought to their notice. The motives which characterize Kohlberg's lower stages are all of this sort: at Stage 1 the avoidance of punishment, at Stage 2 the obtaining of rewards, at Stage 3 the avoidance of disapproval and dislike, at Stage 4 the avoidance of censure by legitimate authorities, and even at Stage 5 the maintenance of respect from the community – all consequences which will accrue to the agent only if his action (or inaction) is publicly noted. But the feelings of guilt, remorse, anxiety and inadequacy which result from the agent's violation of his *own* self-accepted moral principles (on which Stage 6 judgments are based) cannot be escaped, and this is a logical 'cannot'. The principles are *his* principles, indicating obligations which *he* acknowledges as weighing upon him and justifying the doing of X rather than Y. If he then goes ahead and does Y, he knows that as long as he continues to accept the normative authority of those principles self-castigation is inevitable. 'I wouldn't be able to live with myself afterwards' is a typical response of Stage 6 subjects to Kohlberg's moral dilemmas.

However, it would be an over-simplification to draw too stark a contrast between the 'internal', 'self-directed', 'guilt-ethic' motivation of Stage 6, and the 'external', 'other-directed', 'shame-ethic' motivation of Stages 1–5. The shame/guilt distinction is most convincingly portrayed in terms of a continuum, for clearly Stages 1–5 are not all equally 'shame-based'; as Gilligan puts it, 'The middle stages . . . are mixed shame-and-guilt ethics which are transitional between the relatively pure and extreme shame ethic of Stage 1 and the guilt ethic of Stage 6'.[31] Similarly, there is often an 'internal' element in the forms of motivation which characterize the lower stages; the 'external' sanctions of reward, punishment, approval and disapproval may become 'internalized', and thereby operate as motives (and justifications) for action when no source of 'external' authority is present. The concept of 'internalization' is, in any case, a somewhat hazy one, and the 'internal/external' distinction is consequently of limited value for the purposes of the present discussion. Nevertheless, there is still an important sense in which the motivation for moral action at Stage 6 is more guilt-based and less dependent upon sanctions *originating* from 'outside' the agent than it is at the lower stages, and this feature of Stage 6 reasoning entitles us, for the reasons outlined in the previous paragraph, to expect a greater degree of consistency between judgment and action at that stage.

4. Why do Kohlberg's own findings fail to give complete support to his claim that 'true knowledge of principles predicts virtuous action'?

Kohlberg's Platonic view of 'moral knowledge', when allied to the logical features of guilt demonstrated above, might lead one to expect Stage 6 subjects *always* to act in accordance with their 'principled' judgments. Yet Kohlberg's own data show that such subjects do, at times, act against their principles – for example, in continuing to administer increasingly severe electrical shocks to the 'victim' in Milgram's study (if this is admitted as an example of 'inconsistent' as well as 'immoral' action).

Again, moderate internalism offers a formal account of why it is not surprising that 'principled' judgments, though more likely to be acted upon than 'conventional' or 'pre-conventional' ones, are at times overridden in practice. The prospect of suffering guilt and self-castigation is by no means the only motivating influence upon human behaviour. I may know that guilt will be experienced as a result of a particular action which I believe I ought not to do, yet still for other reasons *want* to perform the action so much that the inevitable pangs of self-condemnation become out-weighed or diminished in my estimation; I fail to do that which I believe I ought to do because of the strength of the countervailing factors. Thus, if the Stage 6 subjects who continued to administer shocks in the Milgram experiments were acting contrary to their 'principled' judgments, they must, in practice, have wanted to avoid self-condemnation *less* than they wanted something else (e.g. to avoid the embarrassment of open conflict with the exper-imenter). Such a decision may be sometimes deliberately and consciously made, but probably more often results from allowing one's attention to dwell upon the more immediate situational sanctions and incentives at the expense of the more remote, 'cool-hour', 'principled' considerations. In the Milgram experiments, for example, the subject is faced here and now with the exper-imenter's instructions, demands and apparent expectations, oppo-sition to which will create immediate tension and antagonism, whereas the situation has to be *translated* and *re-interpreted* in terms of moral principles before reflective self-judgment and self-castigation can occur.

This view of 'weak-willed' Stage 6 subjects suggested by the logical features of moderate internalism is supported by some empirical studies which have found relationships between atten-tion and self-control. The ability to attend closely to a task without being distracted has been shown to correlate positively with resist-ance to *moral* temptation (e.g. in a cheating test).[32] Other studies have indicated connections between being able to resist temp-tation and being able to delay the gratification of one's desires (e.g. in choosing a delayed, larger reward in preference to a smaller, immediate one).[33] There are, then, both logical and psychological grounds for attributing 'weak-willed' behaviour at Stage 6 (and presumably at lower stages also) partly to a failure in attention and imagination which causes the subject to allow immediate motivational factors to override more remote justifi-catory ones, despite the fact that the latter are in accord with his 'cool-hour' principles. Whether or not a person will act upon his principles in a particular situation, therefore, will depend not only upon his level of moral reasoning but also upon the way he directs his attention and imagination to the morally relevant features of that situation. *inc. counteravailing factor*

This chapter has presented some conflicting accounts of the logical and empirical relationships between moral judgment and moral action. A form of moderate internalism was proposed as a way of resolving the philosophical dispute between extreme internalism and extreme externalism. Some empirical studies were then considered, resulting from which four key questions were formulated. Finally, these four questions were examined in the light of the explanatory framework offered by moderate internalism, and some answers were suggested which took note of both the logical and empirical dimensions of the issues at stake.

I hope that these tentative probings have not only highlighted the diverse problems surrounding the relationship between moral judgment and moral action, but have also shown that it is not impossible for philosophers and psychologists to explore a common problem jointly and fruitfully. Moral development and its relationship with the judgment/action issue offers an ideal area for such collaboration, the results of which should be considered carefully and critically by moral educators at the chalk-face.

NOTES AND REFERENCES

(1) Frankena, W. F. (1958) 'Obligation and motivation in recent moral philosophy' in Melden, A. I. (ed.) *Essays in Moral Philosophy* (Seattle: University of Washington Press), pp. 40–1.
(2) Plato (1956 edn) *Protagoras*, translated by Guthrie, W. K. C. (Harmondsworth, Middx: Penguin).
(3) Stevenson, C. S. (1937) The emotive meaning of ethical terms, *Mind* **XLVI**, 16.
(4) Hare, R. M. (1952) *The Language of Morals* (Oxford: Clarendon).
(5) Hare, R. M. (1952) *Freedom and Reason* (Oxford: Clarendon).
(6) Gardiner, P. L. (1954–5) On assenting to a moral principle, *Proceedings of the Aristotelian Society* **LV**, 29.
(7) Horsburgh, H. J. N. (1954) The criteria of assent to a moral rule, *Mind* **LXIII**, 349.
(8) Cooper, N. (1971) 'Further thoughts on oughts and wants', in Mortimore, G. W. (ed.) *Weakness of Will* (London: Macmillan), p. 225.

(9)   Piaget, J. (1932) *The Moral Judgment of the Child* (London: Rout-
      ledge), Foreword.
(10) Hartshorne, H. and May, M. A. (1928–30) *Studies in the Nature
      of Character* (New York: Macmillan).
(11) Kohlberg, L. (1969) 'The cognitive-developmental approach to
      socialization' in Goslin, D. A. (ed.) *Handbook of Socialization
      Theory and Research* (Chicago: Rand McNally), p. 394.
(12) Kohlberg, L. (1970) 'Education for justice: a modern statement of
      the Platonic view' in Sizer, T. and Sizer, N. (eds) *Moral Education:
      Five Lectures* (Cambridge, MA: Harvard University Press), p. 64.
(13) Ibid.
(14) Milgram, S. (1974) *Obedience to Authority* (London: Tavistock).
(15) Kohlberg (1969) *op. cit.*, p. 395, and (1970) *op. cit.*, pp. 78–9.
(16) Kohlberg, L., Colby, A., Gibbs, J., Speicher-Dubin, B., and
      Power, C. (1977) *Assessing Moral Stages: A Manual* (Cambridge,
      MA: Harvard University Press).
(17) Huston, T. L., and Korte, C. (1976) 'The responsive bystander' in
      Lickona, T. (ed.) *Moral Development and Behaviour* (New York:
      Holt, Rinehart & Winston), p. 277.
(18) Burton, R. V. (1976) 'Honesty and dishonesty' in Lickona, T. (ed.)
      Moral Development and Behaviour (New York: Holt, Rinehart &
      Winston).
(19) Podd, M. H. (1972) Ego identity status and morality: the relation-
      ship between two developmental constructs, *Developmental Psy-
      chology* **6**, 497–507.
(20) Krebs, R. L. (1967) 'Some relations between moral judgment,
      attention and resistance to temptation'. Unpublished doctoral dis-
      sertation, University of Chicago.
(21) Schwartz, S., Feldman, K., Brown, M., and Heingartner, A. (1969)
      Some personality correlates of conduct in two situations of moral
      conflict, *Journal of Personality* **37**, 41–58.
(22) Kohlberg, L. (1971) 'From Is to Ought' in Mischel, T. (ed.) *Cogni-
      tive Development and Epistemology* (New York: Academic Press).
(23) Mischel, W., and Mischel, H. N. (1976) 'A cognitive social-learning
      approach to morality and self-regulation' in Lickona, T. (ed.)
      Moral Development and Behaviour (New York: Holt, Rinehart &
      Winston).
(24) Blasi, A. (1980) Bridging moral cognition and moral action: a
      critical review of the literature, *Psychological Bulletin* **88**, 37.
(25) Thalberg, I. (1971) 'Acting against one's better judgment' in Morti-
      more, G. W. (ed.) *Weakness of Will* (London: Macmillan), p. 245.
(26) Griffiths, A. P. (1958) Acting with reason, *Philosophical Quarterly*
      VIII, 299.
(27) Blasi (1980) *op. cit.*, p. 20.
(28) Cooper, N. (1968) Oughts and wants, *Proceedings of the Aristote-
      lian Society* **XLII** 152.
(29) Gilligan, J. (1976) 'Beyond morality: psychoanalytic reflections on

shame, guilt and love' in Lickona, T. (ed.) *Moral Development and Behaviour* (New York: Holt, Rinehart & Winston), p. 154.
(30) Kohlberg (1969) *op. cit.*, p. 392.
(31) Gilligan (1976) *op. cit.*, p. 153.
(32) Grim, P. F., Kohlberg, L., and White, S. H. (1968) Some relationships between conscience and attentional processes, *Journal of Personality and Social Psychology* 8, 239–52.
(33) Mischel, W., and Gilligan, C. (1964) Delay of gratification, motivation for the prohibited gratification, and response to temptation, *Journal of Abnormal and Social Psychology* 69, 411–7.

FURTHER QUESTIONS FOR CONSIDERATION

(1) Do you agree with Socrates that 'to make for what one believes to be evil is not in human nature'?
(2) Is insincerity or hypocrisy necessarily involved if one does what one claims to believe is wrong?
(3) Should we be surprised if Kohlberg is right in claiming that 'people's verbal moral values about honesty have nothing to do with how they act'? What exactly is a 'verbal moral value'?
(4) What is 'moral cognition'?
(5) Does 'ought' imply 'might not'?
(6) What is the distinction between shame and guilt? What significance does this have for methods of moral education?
(7) What value might there be in teaching children to 'delay the gratification of their desires'? How might this be attempted?

Chapter 11

Why Act on Kohlberg's Moral Judgments?

This book has tried to demonstrate that what is commonly known as 'the judgment/action issue' is not really a single, unified 'issue' at all, but a rather messy collection of loosely linked problems with which philosophers, psychologists and others have long been concerned – ever since Socrates' provocative claim that to know the Good is to do it. As we saw in Chapter 10, philosophers have busied themselves with questions about the logical relationship between moral judgment and moral action, the emotive, prescriptive and conative features of moral judgment, and the analysis of 'moral weakness'; while more recently psychologists have tried to study the empirical relationship between 'moral cognition' and moral behaviour, and to propose theoretical interpretations of that relationship.

These general concerns have given rise to a host of more specific problems, some of them highlighted by the design of the various psychological research studies and the assumptions lying behind them. Considerable difficulties have arisen in trying to reach agreement over what is to count as a moral judgment and how one is to know whether or not a subject has made one, and over what is to count as a moral action and how one is to know whether or not a subject has performed one.

The conceptual and methodological questions here are closely intertwined, but the logical priority of the former over the latter has not always been realized – we have to be reasonably clear about what it is we are trying to study before we try to study it.

Misleading conclusions can easily be drawn by researchers who fail to respect this logical priority.

'The judgment/action issue' thus becomes an exceedingly complex matter, in that it is constituted by a variety of different problems of logically different kinds. All of these, however, stem from an apparently obvious feature of human life – namely that we all at times fail to do what we think we ought to do. This feature, which has provided the central theme of this book, can be expressed in all sorts of ways; for example, by saying that human beings often fail to act upon their principles or to live up to their ideals, or that they are prone to moral weakness or weakness of will, or that they can at times reveal an inconsistency or gap between their moral reasoning and their behaviour. Various explanatory concepts have been used to account for this phenomenon, ranging from the theologian's 'original sin' through the common-sense notions of 'conscience' and 'character' to the psychologist's 'ego strength'. Attempts to define and explain the relationship between moral judgment and action, then, inevitably lead us into a conceptual minefield. It will be the contention of this chapter that Lawrence Kohlberg has not picked his way with sufficient care in this perilous area.

What has Kohlberg's contribution been here? It is an all-too-common criticism of Kohlberg that he is 'interested only in moral reasoning' and that his theory has nothing to say about moral *action*. A study of his extensive writings shows that this charge is not justified, yet the fact that it is so frequently levelled is perhaps not without significance. Kohlberg's predominant concern clearly *is* with moral reasoning, and it is certainly arguable that he has not said *enough* about moral action. Morality is, by definition, a practical business, for it is about what ought and ought not to be *done*. Of course, a person's reasons and justifications why it ought or ought not to be done are of great moral significance and interest, yet the very concept of morality becomes distorted, even incomprehensible, if undue emphasis is placed upon its 'judgmental' or 'theoretical' aspects. This fundamental point about the nature and function of morality is well underlined by Hare's comment: 'If we were to ask of a person, "What are his moral principles?" the way in which we could be most sure of a true answer would be by studying what he *did*'[1] (italics in original).

Kohlberg's basic approach to the study of morality, however, is in radical disagreement with Hare in this respect. According to Kohlberg, one finds out what a person's moral principles are (or whether he really has anything which Kohlberg would count as moral principles), not by studying how he actually behaves, but by analysing and interpreting his verbal responses to a hypothetical dilemma. Yet, as was argued in Chapter 5, this hypothetical approach has important logical limitations which make it an unreliable guide to what happens in 'real-life morality'. These limitations can be summarized as follows:

1. Moral conflict comes to be construed exclusively as conflict between rival moral principles (such as truth-telling versus promise-keeping, or respect for property versus respect for life). This kind of moral conflict, however, is probably less common empirically and less central logically than is the clash between principle and inclination (when I judge that I *ought* to do X, but do not feel that I *want* to do X).

2. Hypothetical dilemmas necessarily lack that first-hand immediacy which is an essential ingredient of genuine moral experience. In making a real-life moral decision my motives, feelings, wants and emotions may run counter to my hypothetical reasoning and judgments, which will often need to be modified if I actually find myself in such a situation. Direct emotional experience of a situation is a necessary condition of participating in it as a moral agent – and such participation is a very different activity from engaging in a hypothetical ethical debate about the Heinz dilemma.

Kohlberg's methodology, therefore, by its very nature virtually equates moral agency with the making of judgments about hypothetical ethical dilemmas, and this orientation must impose severe limitations on what he can say about morality proper and the real-life business of moral decision-making. In this respect at least Kohlberg simply by-passes 'the judgment/action issue'. However, it would be unfair to suggest that Kohlberg totally ignores the problematic relationship between moral judgment and moral action, for he does occasionally in his voluminous writings address himself to this question. The remainder of this chapter will be devoted to a critical appraisal of this portion of his work.

Kohlberg's claim, in brief, is that the higher the stage of reasoning a subject is at, the more likely is he to act in accordance with his moral judgments, and that consequently 'maturity of moral thought should predict to maturity of moral action'.[2] This is because 'moral judgment determines action by way of concrete definitions of rights and duties in a situation'.[3] The evidence usually cited by Kohlberg to support this conclusion comes from experimental cheating tests, Milgram's obedience studies and an analysis of the Berkeley University sit-in.[4]

This account of 'moral action' is extremely scanty in comparison with the elaborate exposition and interpretation which characterizes Kohlberg's work on moral judgment. It is, in my view, inadequate and obscure in a number of respects; by examining these we may be able to clarify more precisely some of the issues at stake in 'the judgment/action issue'.

1. DRAWING CONCLUSIONS FROM THE EVIDENCE

My first set of objections concerns the sort of evidence to which Kohlberg refers and the conclusions he tries to derive from it. The range of 'moral behaviour' on which he bases his generalizations is very restricted and hardly representative of our everyday experience. Decisions about whether or not to cheat or inflict electric shocks during psychological experiments or to join a university sit-in protest do not represent typical dilemmas with which most moral agents are faced. Indeed, it is doubtful whether the cheating test raises a *moral* issue involving *moral* behaviour in any significant sense at all. As Kohlberg himself says, ' . . . the experimental situation is Mickey Mouse (it does not matter much whether one cheats or not), and . . . it is fishy (the experimenter explicitly leaves the child unsupervised in a situation where one would expect supervision)'.[5] This point is underlined by Hersh, Paolitto and Reimer: 'Experimental cheating tests . . . are one step removed from real-life decisions. Subjects may not know that they are being observed for their cheating behaviour, but they do know they are involved in an experiment and may not attribute much importance to their actions'.[6] But the whole point about moral actions and situations is that importance *is* attributed to them and that they are *not* 'Mickey Mouse', so why should Kohlberg think that he is investigating *moral* behaviour in such experiments?

To draw general conclusions about 'moral action' from such

dubious examples, then, is quite unjustifiable. The moral domain covers a vast area, and it is a complex task to attempt to map out its main contours in terms of its characteristic form and content. The meagre data on which Kohlberg bases his account of 'moral action' cannot begin to do justice to this complexity.

Furthermore, the data as presented cannot for the most part illuminate what Kohlberg appears to think it does, for in order to study the relationship between moral judgment and action we need to know (a) what the subject believed he ought to do, and (b) what he actually did do. Yet in the cheating tests it is *assumed* that subjects always think it wrong to cheat, and in the Milgram study it is *assumed* that subjects always think it wrong to inflict the electric shock; so the percentages which Kohlberg quotes are always of how many Stage X subjects *actually* cheated or gave the shock. But it is perfectly possible that many subjects do *not* believe they ought not to cheat or to give the shock, and are thus showing 'consistency' or 'strength of will' in acting upon their beliefs by cheating or giving the shock; this is particularly likely in the Milgram experiment, where many may believe they ought to keep to the terms of their contract and do what the experimenter asks them to do. Equally, it is possible that some non-cheaters and non-shockers are showing 'inconsistency' or 'weakness of will' in *not* acting (because of some counter-inclination) upon their belief that it is morally *right* to cheat or give the shock in that situation. Kohlberg's percentages tell us nothing about all this, yet that is the information we need in order to clarify the relationship between judgment and action.

Kohlberg, then, fails to distinguish clearly enough between 'consistent action' (where subjects do what *they* judge is the right thing to do) and 'virtuous action' (where subjects do what is *generally considered* to be the right thing to do – by the experimenter at least). It is only studies of 'consistent action' which can help us unravel 'the judgment/action issue', but unfortunately such studies seem to be conspicuous by their absence. Even the Berkeley sit-in analysis was based on *post-hoc* interviews, and asking students a year after the event why they acted as they did, and how they *now* think they perceived the situation *then*, is a very different procedure from trying to establish whether or not they acted as they believed *at the time* they ought to act.

As Kohlberg's data, therefore, can tell us little about either genuine moral action or consistency between judgment and action, his conclusions cannot be relied upon to throw much light upon the issue he claims to be tackling.

2. CHOICES AND REASONS FOR ACTION

My second set of objections concerns a further failure on Kohlberg's part to draw essential distinctions and to specify precisely which aspect of 'the judgment/action issue' he is dealing with. This confusion is well illustrated in his article 'From is to ought', which concludes with a sub-section entitled 'From thought to action'.[7] Kohlberg begins this sub-section, as the title suggests, by discussing how to 'relate moral judgment to moral action' (pp. 226–8), placing his customary reliance upon cheating tests in arguing that 'maturity of moral thought should predict to maturity of moral action' (pp. 228–9). There are immediate problems here over how 'should' should be interpreted, and more seriously over what is meant by 'maturity of moral action' (other than that Kohlberg presumably approves of it); for as Blasi has commented, '. . . at present nobody seems to know the parameters by which to evaluate the degree of maturity specifically in moral action, independently of cognition'.[8] It is difficult to know what Kohlberg is writing about here, particularly as he has in the preceding paragraph stated that there is 'no valid psychological definition of moral behaviour', and that the only differentiating criterion is 'what the people involved think they are doing' (p. 228).

Leaving this difficulty aside, however, we soon find that Kohlberg is not really concerned with moral *action* at all but with moral *choice*, sliding into a discussion of the latter without appearing to realize that there is a crucial distinction to be drawn here, which lies at the very heart of the issue he is supposed to be analysing. He writes, 'Prediction to *action* thus requires that the alternatives are ordered by a hierarchy related to the individual's basic structures. In the case of Stage 4, we could only predict how a subject would *choose* when social order stands clearly on one side and other values on the other, as in civil disobedience' (p. 230, my italics). As another example of how 'stage defines choice', he then refers to 'the principled subject's sensitivity to justice which gives him a reason to not cheat when "law and order" reasons have become ambiguous or lost their force'. The conclusion drawn in the following sentence is that 'moral judgment dispositions influence *action* through being stable cognitive dispositions' (p. 230, my italics).

This passage reveals serious confusion. There is one question about whether 'stage defines *choice*' (for example, does being at Stage 5 rather than 3 affect whether one decides that it is right or wrong to cheat, steal drugs for one's wife, etc.?), and another question about whether 'moral judgment determines *action*' (for example, does being at Stage 5 rather than 3 affect whether one actually behaves as one believes one ought in cheating, stealing drugs for one's wife, etc.?). These questions are logically distinct, and to blur that distinction is to miss the main point of 'the judgment/action issue'.

The confusion arises from the ambiguity of the notions of 'moral choice' and 'moral decision'. These can refer either to:

(a) 'judgmental', 'propositional' choices and decisions *that* it is right or wrong to cheat, steal drugs, etc., or to
(b) 'behavioural', 'action' choices and decisions *to* or *not to* cheat, steal drugs, etc.

It is this distinction which produces the possibility of 'weak-willed' behaviour, which in turn lies at the heart of 'the judgment/action issue', for it is normally considered a not uncommon feature of our moral experience to decide *that* we ought to do X, but to want for various reasons to do Y rather than X, and consequently to decide *to* do Y rather than X.

Why does Kohlberg ignore this distinction and say so little about the topic he claims to be investigating in this passage – 'behaviour which is consistent with an individual's moral principles' (p. 228)? The explanation seems to lie in his failure to probe sufficiently deeply the concept of 'reasons for action'. Yet again, there are crucial distinctions to be drawn here. In cases of 'weak-willed' behaviour it has been argued throughout this book that what appears to be happening is that two different kinds of 'reason for action' are in conflict. The agent accepts that there are good reasons why he ought to do X, yet other reasons are operative upon him in the actual situation which lead him to do Y instead. In other words he sees that factors A, B, C, constitute reasons which *justify* or *require* the doing of X, yet he fails to do

X because factors D, E, F, constitute reasons which *motivate* or *incline* him to do Y – or to put it more simply, we do not always want to do what we believe we ought to do. Reasons for action of a justifying kind, therefore, do not always provide us with reasons for action of a motivating kind.

Kohlberg does not appear to recognize that these different kinds of reason for action can or should be distinguished. In the passage already quoted, in discussing how 'stage defines choice' he states, 'It is the principled subject's sensitivity to justice which gives him a reason to not cheat when "law and order" reasons have become ambiguous or lost their force', and immediately continues, 'We are arguing that moral judgment dispositions influence action . . .' (p. 230). But justice and law and order are *justificatory* considerations, and while these may well define the subject's 'judgmental' choice *that* it is wrong to cheat, they will not necessarily provide a *motivational* 'reason to not cheat' in the actual situation, where counter-inclinations may weigh more heavily when the chips are down.

This confusion between motivation and justification is evident elsewhere in Kohlberg's work. At one point he writes mysteriously of 'the motivational aspect of morality (as) defined by the motive mentioned by the subject in justifying moral action'.[9] At another he produces a table of 'motives for moral action' corresponding to each of the six stages.[10] Yet in none of these cases is Kohlberg really describing *motives* for *action* – that is, reasons which motivate a person actually to *act* in a certain way; what he is describing are verbal justifications of moral judgments – that is, reasons which a person gives to justify why he thinks that it is right to act in a certain way. Again we must conclude that it is Kohlberg's overwhelming methodological emphasis upon moral *judgment* which leads him to equate these fundamentally distinct kinds of 'reason for action'.

3. RULES AND PRINCIPLES

'Reasons for action' are also connected with a further oddity in Kohlberg's account, which concerns his view of rules and principles. Higher-stage subjects, who are allegedly more likely to act in accordance with their judgments than lower-stage ones, are said to reason in terms of principles rather than rules; 'morally mature men are governed by the principle of justice rather than by a set of rules'.[11] So principles appear to have a stronger, more reliable 'motivational power' than rules:

> The motivational power of principled morality does not come from rigid commitment to a concept or a phrase. Rather, it is motivated by awareness of the feelings and claims of the other people in the moral situation. What principles do is to sort out these claims, without distorting them or cancelling them out, so as (to) leave personal inclination as the arbiter of action.[12]

What precisely distinguishes a rule from a principle in Kohlberg's view? We are told:

> Justice is not a rule or a set of rules, it is a moral principle. By a moral principle we mean a mode of choosing which is universal, a rule of choosing which we want all people to adopt in all situations. We know it is all right to be dishonest and steal to save a life because it is just . . . . We know it is sometimes right to kill, because it is sometimes just. . . . There are exceptions to rules, then, but no exception to principles. . . . A moral principle is not only a rule of action but a reason for action.[13]

This passage raises a host of questions, many of which fall strictly outside the scope of this chapter. Does Kohlberg, for example, grant too high and exclusive a status to 'the principle of justice', placing it at the apex of a Platonic hierarchy, where 'there are not many virtues but one', because 'the good is justice'?[14] Why can we not describe Stage 4 reasons as based on *principles* concerning the maintenance of law, authority and social order? Does Kohlberg really mean that moral principles are *universal* ('rules of choosing which we want all people to adopt in all situations') rather than *universalizable* in Hare's much more sophisticated sense? Who are the 'we' who all 'know' that it is sometimes all right to be dishonest, steal and even kill? Considerable strength of will is required to drop the pursuit of these tempting quarries.

There are, however, quite enough problems lurking in the principle/rule distinction as Kohlberg propounds it and in the relevance he implies that it has for 'the judgment/action issue'. Kohlberg's distinction is obscurely expressed and is made no clearer by his description of a moral principle as a *rule* of choosing and also a *rule* of action; the distinction between a rule of action and a reason for action goes unexplained; and the ambiguity of 'choosing' and of 'a reason for action' is again ignored.

Let us try to dispel some of this conceptual murk. What characterizes a principle and distinguishes it from a rule (as we normally understand these terms) is not its content or its 'universality', but its function. Principles represent sets of highly general considerations which we *appeal to* in order to *justify* a particular course of action in a particular situation.[15] Rules, on the other hand, prescribe more specifically what is or is not to be done in that situation. In terms of content, therefore, there is room for possible overlap between rules and principles: truth-telling or promise-keeping, for instance, could count either as rules in situations where they function simply as prescriptions (as in the rules for witnesses in a court of law, summarized in the oath), or as principles if they are appealed to as a source of justification (as in an argument about the rights and wrongs of gazumping).

If principles, then, are essentially justificatory in nature, they do not have any *necessary* 'motivational power', for the reasons given in the previous subsection, and when Kohlberg claims that 'a moral principle is not only a rule of action but a reason for action', he can be referring only to a *justifying* 'reason for action' of the kind that is involved in the making of 'judgmental', 'propositional' choices and decisions. Principles cannot, therefore, be relied upon to bridge the judgment/action gap. We understand what is meant by expressions like 'He acted against his principles', and do not feel that we are talking logical or psychological nonsense when we use them.

'Having principles' is no guaranteed defence against succumbing to counter-inclinations. As Neil Cooper puts it, 'There is no necessary one-one correlation between the order of priority of a man's moral principles and the order of strength of his desires'.[16] This is because moral principles have a 'cool-hour' quality: 'a man's moral principles are those of his principles of action which in a cool hour he is least prepared to abandon belief in, however much he may be tempted to deviate from them in the heat of the moment'.[17] These important conceptual points show clearly why principles are an appropriate medium through which to describe some central features of Kohlberg's theory, for the discussion of *hypothetical* moral dilemmas is very much a 'cool-hour' activity. But it is in the heat of the moment that one has to choose or decide *to* act or *not to* act upon one's judgments, and here at the heart of 'the judgment/action issue' the role of principles becomes much more problematic than Kohlberg appears to realize.

The aim of this chapter has not been to show that Kohlberg is wrong in his claim that higher-stage subjects are more likely to act in accordance with their judgments than lower-stage subjects. Indeed, the previous chapter tried to show that there are logical considerations which support this claim. Kohlberg's suggestion that 'attention' correlates with 'strength of will'[18] could also be a fruitful one, but I have not referred to this aspect of Kohlberg's work in this chapter as it appears unrelated to his basic, cognitive-developmental interpretation of 'the judgment/action issue'.

What this chapter has shown is that Kohlberg pays scant attention to the complex relationship between moral judgment and moral action. He is prevented from getting to grips with these complexities, partly by the constraints of his 'hypothetical' research method and partly by the inadequacy and undifferentiated nature of his conceptual armoury. Whether or not 'cognitive definitions determine behaviour', as Kohlberg maintains, his own 'cognitive definitions' of moral agency, choices, decisions and principles have certainly determined and restricted his behaviour as an investigator of the moral domain.

It would, however, be churlish to end this chapter and this book on such a note. Kohlberg's work has stimulated teachers and philosophers, educationists and psychologists (as well as children) to think harder about the nature of morality, the development of our moral judgments and possible ways of furthering that development. Without his stimulus there would be far less current concern and informed debate in many countries about moral education and moral development. In particular, his work has thrown into sharp relief the relationship between beliefs and behaviour, which has dominated this book. Disagreement and controversy will doubtless continue to surround that relationship, but the moral and educational problems that stem from it will remain – at least until the day when all can confidently claim that they always behave exactly as they believe they ought.

NOTES AND REFERENCES

(1) Hare, R. M. (1952) *The Language of Morals* (Oxford: Clarendon) p. 1.
(2) Kohlberg, L. (1971) 'From is to ought: how to commit the naturalistic fallacy and get away with it in the study of moral development' in Mischel, T. (ed.) *Cognitive Development and Epistemology* (New York: Academic Press), p. 228.
(3) Ibid., p. 229.
(4) See e.g. Kohlberg, L. (1969) 'Stage and sequence: the cognitive-developmental approach to socialization' in Goslin, D. A. (ed.) *Handbook of Socialization Theory and Research* (Chicago: Rand McNally), pp. 395–6.
(5) Kohlberg, L. (1971) *op. cit.*, p. 229.
(6) Hersh, R. H., Paolitto, D. P. and Reimer, J. (1979) *Promoting Moral Growth* (New York: Longman), p. 96.
(7) Kohlberg, L. (1971) *op. cit.*, pp. 226–32.
(8) Blasi, A. (1980) Bridging moral cognition and moral action: a critical review of the literature, *Psychological Bulletin* **88**(1), 8.
(9) Kohlberg, L. (1963) The development of children's orientation toward a moral order, *Vita Humana* **6**, 13.
(10) Kohlberg, L. (1969) *op. cit.*, pp. 381–2.
(11) Kohlberg, L. (1970) 'Education for justice: a modern statement of the Platonic view' in Sizer, T. and Sizer, N. (eds.) *Moral Education: Five Lectures* (Cambridge, MA: Harvard University Press), p. 70.
(12) Kohlberg, L. (1971) *op. cit.*, p. 231.
(13) Kohlberg, L. (1970) *op. cit.*, pp. 69–70.
(14) Ibid., p. 70.
(15) See Peters, R. S. (1981) *Moral Development and Moral Education* (London: Allen & Unwin).
(16) Cooper, N. (1971) 'Oughts and wants' in Mortimore, G. W. (ed.) *Weakness of Will* (London: Macmillan), p. 197.
(17) Ibid.
(18) Kohlberg, L. (1969) *op. cit.*, pp. 396–7.

FURTHER QUESTIONS FOR CONSIDERATION

(1) Do we discover a person's moral principles by studying what he does, as Hare suggests?
(2) What could be meant by 'maturity of moral action'?
(3) What do you understand by 'moral choice'?
(4) Is 'consistency' of action (with judgment) always a desirable goal? Should moral education always aim at such consistency, regardless of what the judgment is?
(5) How would you distinguish between rules and principles?
(6) Do principles have a 'cool-hour' quality? Is it appropriate to speak of children 'having principles'?

Name Index

Subject Index